Ironic

Alanis Morissette

THE STORY

Ironic

Alanis Morissette

THE STORY

by
barry grills

For Hugh Chandler
and for Nancy

First published in Great Britain by Quartet Books Limited in 1997
A member of the Namara Group
27 Goodge Street
London W1P 2LD

First published in Canada by Quarry Press Inc., 1997

Ironic: The Story of Alanis Morissette is a serious biographical and critical study of Alanis Morissette's career and her lyrics. The quotation of songs written by Alanis Morissette and copyright by her publishers is intended to illustrate the biographical or critical information presented by the author and thus constitutes fair use under existing copyright conventions. Every effort has been made to notify the publisher of these songs that the lyrics have been quoted in this context by the author.

The author gratefully acknowledges the fundamental work of Paul Cantin in chronicling the life of Alanis Morissette first published as "What You Oughta Know" in the *Ottawa Sun* and later at http://www.canoe.ca/JamMusic Alanis, copyright the *Ottawa Sun* and Canoe Limited Partnership, 1996.

A catalogue record for this book is available from the British Library.

ISBN 0 7043 8062 5

Design by Susan Hannah.
Front cover photo by Andrew Wallace, taken during a concert on Alanis Morissette Day in Ottawa, courtesy of CANAPRESS Photo Service.

Printed in Canada by AGMV/Marquis Imprimiere Inc.,
Cap-Saint-Ignace, Quebec.

Contents

Life has a funny way of sneaking up on you.

— *Alanis Morissette*

Pleasant as it is to adapt oneself to one's environment and to the spirit of the times, the pleasures of integrity are greater and more lasting.

— *Hermann Hesse*

Alanis

·Foreword·

I just wanna say that most people's growth is done in private, an artist's growth is done in public. And I thank Canada, the country, for accepting that in me.

— *Alanis Morissette*

Well life has a funny way of sneaking up on you
When you think everything's okay
and everything's going right
And life has a funny way of helping you out when
You think everything's gone wrong
and everything blows up
In your face

— *Ironic*

By the time Alanis Morissette appeared on stage to perform her song *Ironic* at the 25th anniversary of the Canadian Juno Awards at Copps Coliseum in Hamilton, Ontario, on March 10, 1996, there was in the crowd an air of anti-climax. Rock 'n' roll's newest legend had already appeared in the flesh, marching up on stage several times, a real person and not a myth, to accept five Juno Awards acknowledging her arrival as an artist and the success of the album JAGGED LITTLE PILL, which has sold more than fifteen million copies worldwide. Anti-climactic because the sigh of relief was over. Yes, it was true. And, yes, she was here. The first Canadian woman to top the iconographic *Billboard* charts was back home to pick up the industry hardware of her musical homeland. Anti-climactic too because she had already won four Grammy Awards just a few weeks earlier and Canadians just can't quite get over their tendency to be mystified when a fellow citizen finds a place in the sun outside the shade cast by that giant cultural Galacticus known as the United States. Nor can they get over the pout which inevitably follows their surprise, the one which considers it naughty to get too big for your britches.

Emcee Anne Murray introduced Morissette's performance of *Ironic* by detailing her amazing year and by describing her as "perhaps the most honest voice to ever come out of Ottawa," leaving it to the audience and millions of viewers to sort out the thrust of this political-artistic double entendre. And there she was with her band, moving out on stage in her trademark leather pants and billowing one-buttoned blouse, long, dark hair trying frantically to keep up, restless to get going during the more subdued opening lines of the song — "An old man turned ninety-eight / He won the lottery and died the next day" — then suddenly uncorking as she sings the chorus:

> It's like rain on your wedding day
> It's a free ride when you've already paid
> It's the good advice that you just didn't take
> Who would've thought ... it figures.
>
> — *Ironic*

Amid cries of approval from thousands of music fans jammed into the coliseum, she prowled across the stage, nearly driving the hand-held camera crew into retreat.

Anti-climactic on the surface of it. Even considering how Morissette leads the charge of young female musicians whose blunt lyrics have given them the name "the angry young women of rock" — or even considering how an earlier generation of blunt and angry musicians, women and men, have turned over the rock-poetry baton to Alanis and her set — the feeling was anti-climactic. The Grammys again, getting there ahead of the Junos scant days before. Annie Lennox on stage accepting a Grammy and acknowledging her excitement over the numbers of young women now leading the musical charge. Millions of people watching while Alanis Morissette rises to her feet in the audience to give Lennox what appears to be a single-handed standing ovation. Anti-climactic, too, because in Canada she sings about irony, while, scant days earlier, during her performance on the Grammy Awards, she intrigues the audience with an acoustic version of JAGGED LITTLE PILL's first hit single, *You Oughta Know*, the offending word "fuck" bleeped from American television screens and left intact back home in Canada as she voices her anger, bitterness, and even, at times, her retribution over a love affair gone sour.

And, yes, there has been a women's movement in alternative music in recent years which Morissette has ushered into the cultural mainstream with JAGGED LITTLE PILL It's an expression of personal outrage on the heels of power feminism, a post-power feminism, if you will, which retreats from duplicating all that has been wrong with men to a point where it celebrates even womanhood's anguish and pain as part of the human experience, an experience, yes ironically, shared by both sexes. It's still feminist; it still rises out of a state of oppression. But it doesn't ostracize one sex from the other, doesn't maintain that one sex's emotional angst is any different or more severe than the other's.

In other words, there's something happening here. And it certainly isn't anti-climax. In fact, it's irony. Never mind the great debate promulgated by detractors of Morissette who seem to hang a great deal of their argument on the lyrics to *Ironic* and how they're not truly ironic. Never mind all of that. We're talking an entire generation which has found some kind of solace in irony and we're perhaps talking an entire age which will be viewed, if we ever claw our way out of the current morass to where we can look at it objectively, the age of irony.

While watching the Juno Awards that initial sensation of anti-climax evaporates in the face of all the irony which punctuates each performance, loiters under every coliseum seat and intrudes on each applauding palm. The irony is powerful — and tragically self-diffusing. It is up to Alanis Morissette and a cluster of outraged female peers to bring home a motivational conclusion from the power of all that irony — to a generation which recognizes the irony but hasn't yet come up with a conclusion — before the irony gobbles itself up like a snake devouring its own tail.

As writer Rick Salutin said in his column in a December issue of *The Globe & Mail* while examining a trait of the young today towards an "ironic mindset" with respect to the media, "For my part, I wonder how far you can go on an ironic mindset. If *everything* is ironic, you end up pretty harmless, since if it's all equally ironic, why bother trying to change any of it — which is pretty ironic for a subversive. You're drawn into the mainstream willy-nilly since you accept, albeit scornfully, its premises. . . . You can't do much subverting without an alternate model of how things might be, but then you'd *believe* in something and that's so unironic. Irony often comes, it seems to me, from not wanting to have your hopes or dreams dashed. One reason Michael Moore (filmmaker, *Roger and Me, TV Nation*) really is subversive, is that he believes our world could be different; he's not just saying screw you, his little smile conceals the fact that he can picture a whole other kind of society than this. But Moore comes from the 1960s generation and his beliefs are rooted in some sort of left-wing socialism, even if he doesn't talk about it much. I don't deny how difficult it is for people who grew up in the Reagan-Thatcher-Mulroney era to believe another kind of society is possible. But I think this may be a case where an older generation has something to offer a younger."

What has this to do with Alanis Morissette? Simply this: that she has been designated heir apparent to that cultural responsibility of moral outrage which coalesces the young by the music generation which preceded her. She has been lauded as the biggest musical attraction since The Beatles — unfortunately, this comparison comes up frequently with musical acts as if this benchmark alone will lift someone out of some ill-defined cluster of mediocrity — and she has been compared to the late Jim Morrison, as a poet and revolutionary voice for her generation. She has presented herself, without apology and without rancour — "I just wanna say that most people's growth is done in private, an artist's growth is done in public; and I thank Canada, the country, for accepting that in me" — as an artistic fugitive from her Canadian musical past, as an "honest voice," at last achieving the artistic integrity she apparently has always sought.

And whether the lyrics to her smash hit single *Ironic* are truly ironic or just a paean to the edicts of Murphy's Law is not the issue. The issue is that she is reaching an entire generation of young people who exist in a closet of irony with a door so narrowly ajar: the real danger, as Salutin points out, is that any movement to change will be impotent before it gets started, diffused by its own lack of alternative. And, like it or not, when the cultural mainstream reaches out and tugs even the most honest voice from the fringes into a state of superstardom it diffuses the raw, subversive energy by transforming its ethic into, yes, irony. The musical generation preceding Morissette's knows all about it. It's in the invisible ink used to write on the baton of encouragement and congratulations Morissette received when later in the year she played Hyde Park in the company of The Who, with Roger Daltrey and Peter Townshend now talkin' about *her* generation.

The story of Alanis Morissette, therefore, is more than the story of a precocious young woman with talent and focus in abundance who emerged from Ottawa to enjoy phenomenal worldwide music success before the age of twenty-two, who struggled to achieve a self-proclaimed artistic integrity. It's the story of an entire raft of outspoken women and the generation of young people looking for a solution to a feeling of irony so powerful the solution itself may be impossible to detect. It's even the story of an earlier generation of poets and superstars and musical movements which, as Salutin suggests, may have something to offer their younger counterparts, although perhaps they also have much to account for.

So isn't it ironic?

Rehearsal day at the 1996 Juno Awards. A limousine pulls up at the rear entrance where a security guard is ushering the performers in through the back door, controlling traffic, ensuring that their vehicles do not move inside. Briefly, the security guard is challenged by the singing superstar's father, Alan Morissette, who insists that he wants to take the car inside. Politely the security guard stands his ground and ultimately wins his point. Alanis herself, apparently more agreeable, even aloof of the issue and the results of the debate, emerges and, with an almost serene self-possession, enters by way of the door through which she has been directed.

And isn't it ironic that after her performance on the Juno Awards, a line-up of Canadian musical personalities forms to seek her autograph, acknowledging not only her musical success but the heights of popularity she has achieved in scarcely a year? Her autograph includes the peace sign, as if carelessly dotting the "i" in her last name, a bridge perhaps between her generation and its predecessor, an irony itself perhaps that what was embarked upon in the decade thirty years before has yet to be achieved.

And so on it goes, symbolic ironies sprinkled as if from a pepper shaker all over the Canadian gala known as the Juno Awards, if not a perfect launching point for the story of Alanis Morissette, at least an appropriate setting in which to wonder about the ironies of musical superstardom itself, the way, as Morissette sings so often, "life has a funny way of sneaking up on you." Because this 25th anniversary of the awards features in film clips, live performances and as guest presenters an outstanding assemblage of former Canadian stars who seem to have gathered to hand over the crown to the leader of the next generation of superstar. Never mind that Zal Yanovsky, former guitarist with The Lovin' Spoonful and one of five new members of the Juno Hall of Fame, along with guitar magician Dominic Troiano, the leather-clad old alternative rock star John Kay of Steppenwolf, Denny Doherty of The Mamas and The Papas, and David Clayton

Thomas of Blood, Sweat & Tears, feels dishonest accepting the award after having been out of the music business for twenty-five years. They're all still there to demonstrate that, while the times they are a-changin', they haven't changed that much at all.

Paul Anka, presented singing *Havin' My Baby* in one of many film clips acknowledging twenty-five years of Canadian musical development, like Morissette, is from Ottawa. Like Morissette as well, he's returned to Ottawa to feel, at times, that cold shoulder from which he once moved away, victimized by that uniquely Canadian resistance to Canadians who achieve global success instead of staying home to reinforce a kind of peculiar and insular Canadian reverse snobbery.

All of these ironies lollygag in the air as Morissette stalks on stage to mesmerize the audience. And, yes, there is just a glimpse of the ghost of Jim Morrison hovering nearby, not in the sheen of her trademark leather pants which resembles the sheen of *his* trademark leather pants, but in the raw force of the lyrics and in the darkly abandoned stage presence, that apparently in-your-face refusal to compromise.

No wonder the story of Alanis Morissette is much more than the story of a precocious artist who decided at a startlingly young age to become a singing star. It's the story of irony and outrage and telling it bluntly, of picking up the baton of artistic integrity and marching with it into the hopes and frustrations of an entire generation. Life, after all, is a story. And life, indeed, has a funny way of sneaking up on you.

Live at the Juno Awards.

·one·

Perfect

Dear Mr. Gorman, just think you've taught me all I know, and I'll never swallow gum again . . . Hey, Mr. G. watch 4 me. Love, Alanis.

— *Alanis Morissette*

Be a good girl
You've got to try a little harder
That simply wasn't good enough
To make us proud

— *Perfect*

It goes without saying that we take with us wherever we go the impact on our personalities and creativity of the location and circumstances of where we grew up. The same is true of Alanis Morissette. To know a little more about Morissette, one has to know a little more about Ottawa, especially its personality as the capital of a sprawling nation dedicated to the homespun creeds of duty, hard work and, more importantly, moral motherhood and apple pie. Ottawa is a kind of shrunken microcosm of Canada itself, but with a twist reflecting the fact it is the city which seeks to operate the nation. You either come out of Ottawa cold, cowed, and complacent or you emerge spitting in everyone's face. This isn't because the city is Ottawa per se. Rather, it's because Ottawa is a federal capital and, as such, tends to be a mean parent. Government seats, as mean parents these days, show a ritual proclivity to be punitive, demanding, and self-centered. It wants all of its citizens to grow up just like it has, towing the line, not rocking the boat, participating in the edification of a corporately useful, but fatuous acceptance of the greedy status quo so that the whole system churns profitably and securely down the rails. Western civilization's capital cities have a tendency this decade to embrace the two necessary psychological components of a free market society, namely envy and contempt. Like Washington. Like London. Like Paris, Rome, and Bonn. It's as Freudian as the first time you were instructed on how to set the table for dinner, ego slammed by super-ego. As Morissette sings in *Perfect*, "With everything I do for you / The least you can do is keep quiet." She may be talking about parents. She may be talking about Ottawa. But judging by the tremendous response to her music and lyrics, the apparent identification her audience feels, she's probably talking about all those youthful victims which spew out of the grinder when opportunity is legislated into the hands of a shrinking, privileged few.

On the surface of it, at least, there's a kind of comfort in all that order. The Parliament buildings are perched on a hill which, at first glance, conveys a sturdy permanence resembling Mount Rushmore. Not far away, in the winter months, blissful, healthy, cherubic families skate the Rideau Canal. During the spring there's a tulip festival. All year long, there are a seemingly endless array of parks in which to jog, walk the dog, and ignore your neighbors, while, scattered all around, are the sprawling and secure suburbs where the barbecues spit and the swimming pools gurgle. It seems nice. It seems safe. It promotes a state of calm *okay*.

But the same could be said of Toronto where Morissette lived for a while, or even sections of Los Angeles where she lives now. The similarities are on the surface. Underneath, that's where you get to the differences, the twists. If Los Angeles is a photographic coffee table book about the palace of Versailles, then Toronto is an applied psychology text, a sort of *I'm Okay, You're Okay* tranquilizer, while Ottawa, underneath the parental sternness, is a political survival manual.

Under the skin of it all, Ottawa is a powerful place. But there's an equally powerful insecurity lurking underneath all that influence. Its population comes and goes, generally speaking. You don't hear "born and raised" in Ottawa as much as you do in other places. More often you hear "moved to and left" because of the transitory nature of politics and all the bureaucratic institutions which politics puts in place and then takes away again. People may win elections to go to Ottawa but they often lose them, too, so that they have to leave. And because power corrupts, some people enter Ottawa an idealist and are kicked out again just another cynic. Born and *razed* in Ottawa perhaps seems a more appropriate way to put it.

No wonder, when one considers the impact Morissette is having on a generation of young people, the way her lyrics are reaching out to them, Ottawa and what it represents reflects a powerful symbol of numb disenfranchisement to her and to them. "At a time when teens and twentysomethings are going in for multiple piercings and tattoos just to *feel* something, is it any wonder Morissette's angry growl would catch on?" mused David Hochman in *Entertainment Weekly's* brief tribute to Morissette during its Best of 1996 round-up. The "angry growl" may not be politically-motivated per se, but it's all connected to that feeling of disenfranchisement today's young people must endure. The fact that Morissette emerged from a federal capital which, along with many other federal capitals at the helm of western civilization, continues to compromise that sense of citizenship we all need to enhance our personal worth, adds a powerful poignance to the identification her audience finds in her lyrics.

Morissette is from the same generation that has been compromised by western civilization's move towards balance sheets and profits which, ultimately, dehumanizes individuals by defining them solely by their cost and economic function. When Morissette lunges out on stage to shout out her complaint about corporate music executives in her song *Right Through You* —

Wait a minute man
You mispronounced my name
You didn't wait for all the information
Before you turned me away

— there's an entire generation of helpless victims to share her angst and frustration, their names mispronounced as well, shut out by a system concerned with nothing more than their societal cost. Whether unconsciously or not, Alanis Morissette has lived intimately within a federal capital where someone is trying to implement the disenfranchisement modern political trends seem to insist upon.

But there is more about Ottawa in the story of Alanis Morissette, a characteristic about the city which it shares to some extent with Canada itself. And that's the tendency to turn a cold shoulder towards its musical artists when they achieve staggering success on a world stage. Sometimes coming back home can be difficult. It was in Ottawa that local radio stations showed a strong reticence to play music from JAGGED LITTLE PILL in the early days, apparently not approving of the singer's development from pop dance singer to blunt alternative rock star. *Ottawa Citizen* music writer Norman Provencher addressed the topic as early as August 1995, when he took a small "g" gonzo look at the local radio stations' ambivalence about Morissette. Conceding that Morissette didn't need any help from his newspaper, that, indeed, she had "pony-tailed business thugs from L.A. to New York ready, willing, and able" to take care of business, not to mention a record company CEO, Madonna, who "can and has kicked some major butt in her time" to ensure she was getting a fair shake on the radio waves, he did, apologetically — "normally we'd rather poke needles in our eyes than be accused of homerism"— look into the situation.

"Is commercial radio in Ottawa ignoring what's arguably the hottest phenomenon in North American popular music, Morissette's JAGGED LITTLE PILL album?" he mused. "It kind of depends on who you ask. Some fans and Morissette's record company think radio stations have taken a puzzling attitude towards the album. The stations contend that the album, and particularly the first single, *You Oughta Know,* slips and slides between all of their demographic criteria. So far only Energy 1200 has had the song in any sort of regular rotation, although KOOL-FM has recently come on board. After that, the hair-splitting becomes a little dizzying. CHEZ's 'classic rock' apparently precludes anything too 'alternative.' The Bear, allegedly the home of the tougher stuff, has taken a pass on the single because the intro is too dance-y, whatever that might mean. It all seems a little arbitrary and doctrinaire, although we are not, it must be conceded, radio pros."

After reviewing JAGGED LITTLE PILL's various successes so far, he suggested "It's in the area of radio play and perhaps demand that the True North and the States part company. American listeners are just pigs over the girl. As our Texas correspondent Greg Barr noted last month, *You Oughta Know* has owned the alternative-rock charts for weeks and has crossed over strongly onto something called 'active rock' charts. In the critical world of video, Alanis is a complete darling on both sides of the border. Trendsetters MTV just love her. Canada's Much is also smitten and the video for the single is in heavy rotation and number one on the request line. Even on notoriously picky MusiquePlus — which, to be fair, has a mandate to promote French-language material — Alanis is a strong No. 3 on the lines.

"To listen to the station execs tell it, programming is listener-driven, a rough set of guidelines that allow programmers to winnow their way through the tonnes of product that tumbles over their transoms every week. But how could that really be true, in the face of the numbers of Alanis and others who've sold truckloads of product before ever seeing the light of day on Canadian radio? No, we hate to say it, but our strong suspicion remains that we're all being fed a bunch of favorites compiled by people who think they know what people are thinking. And if something as large as the Morissette album falls through the cracks, what else are we missing?" he asked.

Nor did the Ottawa controversy over Morissette ease up significantly as JAGGED LITTLE PILL vaulted her into superstardom. By March of the following year, Toronto newspapers were reporting in detail that Morissette was not appreciated by everyone in her home town. And even the reticence of Ottawa radio stations was still making news.

"Four-time Grammy winner Alanis Morissette will get the keys to her hometown Friday, but not without some backbiting and slagging from some of the people she left behind," reported Mark Bourrie in the *Toronto Star*. "When Ottawa's city council decided earlier this year on the honor, city newspapers were flooded with dozens of letters from people offended by what they called the obscene lyrics on her hit album, JAGGED LITTLE PILL. . . . Egos in Ottawa's music scene have been bruised by remarks that Morissette, 21, has made to American entertainment writers. In the fall, she told *Spin* magazine that 'I've had people cheat me out of a lot of money. I think it is my tuition to the College of Music Career.' She also told the *Baltimore Sun* that people in Ottawa's music business had repressed her creativity, making her early song writing a 'black and white task.'

"Leading the charge against Morissette in Ottawa is the satirical magazine *Frank*," reported Bourrie, "which ranked her seventh in 'The Bores of '95.' She's a 'shrewish bobbysoxer (who) has grown too big for her bridgework,' *Frank* said. At Glebe Collegiate, where Morissette went to high school, students still listen every morning to the former dance music diva's version of *O Canada* piped into classrooms. A number yesterday dismissed it as 'bubble gum.' Glebe students are skeptical of the litany of misery that runs through JAGGED LITTLE PILL. While at high school, Morissette was working on her first two dance music albums. 'This is the most affluent high school in the city,' said one Grade 12 student. 'All the time she was here, everyone fawned over her and treated her like a little queen,' she said. 'Alanis would be out at night with [NHL star] Alexandre Daigle or hanging around with Caroline Mulroney [daughter of former Canadian Prime Minister Brian Mulroney] at some dance club, then be back at school, where everyone would fawn all over her.'"

In an article by Anne McIlroy published in *The Globe & Mail* in Toronto just four days later, a similar analysis of Ottawa's reaction to its stars was reported, as well as Morissette's philosophical response. Admitting "Ottawa is truly the capital of a country known for spurning its successful sons and daughters," McIlroy said, "When it [JAGGED LITTLE PILL] was released, many Ottawa stations didn't give it much air time, claiming the album, which has been described as vitriolic, didn't fit their demographics. Many critics slammed it. When Mayor Jacquelin Holzman announced plans to award Ms. Morissette the key to the city, a local television show was flooded with calls from residents registering their anger. But the mayor bravely went ahead and proclaimed yesterday [March 8] Alanis Morissette Day. Ms. Morissette, 21, was gracious in her acceptance."

Announcing an upcoming Canadian tour at the press conference, Morissette also commented on the nature of fame and anger. "I just want to make peace with where I come from," she said. Wrote McIlroy, "She said she understands why some people in Ottawa, including some at her old high school, Glebe Collegiate, don't like her new work. When she left Ottawa she was a child star, a clean-cut young woman who launched her career in bubble-gum dance pop. 'I don't think it is just Canada. I think it is humans. You know, I think there are some people who have difficulty with other people's success. That's part of life. I don't think it is just Glebe.'" And she stressed that she still had the support of her parents, despite the nature of some of her material.

"They are pretty cool about it, you know. I'm sort of apologetic in the sense that I knew what I was getting into and I knew there was a price to be paid for releasing my record. I never want either my siblings or my parents to have to pay that price because it wasn't their choice. It wasn't their career choice," said Morissette.

Maybe it's just humans, but maybe it's Ottawa too and maybe it's Canada. When Morissette returned to Ottawa later in the year to perform at the Corel Centre on August 9, there were newspaper reviews which seemed nothing more than an earnest search for any excuse to bring her down a peg or two. And one of those reviews came courtesy of the same Norman Provencher who had been concerned about her lack of radio play when JAGGED LITTLE PILL was first released.

"Depending on how you do the math, Alanis Morissette has spent something like 500 nights on the road since releasing JAGGED LITTLE PILL on a large unsuspecting public 16 months ago," wrote *Ottawa Citizen* writer Provencher. "So, the point is, you'd think she would have learned to play that stupid harp by now. Because, and again it still depends on your ciphering, she's played *All I Really Want* (which opened Friday night's show at the Corel Centre and the half dozen shows we've seen so far) maybe 500 times and it still is the worst darn honking we've heard in our lives. Which brings us to the moral of our story here: there's definitely an art-meets-science-meets-showbiz aspect to Ottawa's Ms. Thing that has to be dealt with before we go one step further.

"Look, maybe we're being unfair. She's working with a first album, she's now 22 years old, and maybe we really shouldn't be demanding E-Street Band-level performances every time out. But, she's dealing with a curse and a blessing here. The blessing is her album JAGGED LITTLE PILL has sold something like 15 million copies worldwide and hasn't slowed down one instant since they took it out of the box. That's also the curse because she's been performing the same material for more than a year and, frankly, apart from the snazzy new video stuff behind her from time to time, we very well might be approaching critical Morissette mass here.

"Don't get us wrong. Everything happened when and how it should have last night before about 12,500 fans at the Corel Centre. Every single song leapt into the crowd's face and, say, during *Hand In My Pocket*, all of the audience appreciation requirements were met (as the crowd mimicked lyrics like 'Hailing a taxi cab . . . lighting a cigarette . . . , etc). But, and this could well just be the view from here, there may be a bump showing. It could very well be from touring every night for more than 14 months but, all of a sudden, there's a formula happening that get's a little irritating after awhile.

"Don't misunderstand, this is still one of the most powerful and, forgive us, uplifting shows we're likely to see this or any year. But, maybe the thing is, she only has the one album to work with. As good as most of the songs are, there is a limit somewhere and it's getting close," said Provencher.

What a difference six months makes! Provencher and fellow *Citizen* writer Carolyn Abraham had put together a detailed profile and history of Morissette for a February 24 edition of the newspaper which featured the ruminations of Max Keeping, a well-known newsman with CJOH Television in Ottawa and a booster of the young superstar from an early age. "Keeping, the hometown cheerleader who has chronicled Morissette's rise and visited her twice on tour, dreads that 'the Paul Anka syndrome' is striking the city once again. 'Paul Anka came back and he was snubbed. Even when he tried to come back, when the Senators [hockey team] arrived, he was treated miserably. I'm hoping that will never happen to another artist, and yeah, I'm starting to hear some of the negatives about Alanis already . . . it's so wrong.'"

But so Canadian. This is not to say that Canadian music pundits, when writing about a musical superstar should be awed into submission because she's a Canadian, or turn a blind eye to what in their act might need continued development. It is to say, however, that sometimes the witch hunt for flaws gets a little tangential and the Canadian slap on the wrist a little too patronizing.

Ironic that Max Keeping should bring up Paul Anka. Except that when one wishes to marry Morissette's development as an artist to the personality of her home town, country, era, and environment, the way one must do with any artist, it isn't surprising in the least that Paul Anka rises to the surface of the examination. Keeping is merely alluding to the logical comparisons which must be made between the local superstar of today and the local superstar of yesterday. And the comparisons are there. In fact it is more than appropriate to glance briefly at Ottawa's other musical star whose career has spanned nearly four decades, a period in which he has amassed worldwide record sales, according to *The New Rolling Stone Encyclopedia of Rock & Roll*, in excess of 100 million copies.

Born in Ottawa on July 30, 1941, Paul Anka first began to perform as a singer and impersonator when he was age 10. The son of a Lebanese restaurateur, he recorded as early as 15 years of age, after his father paid for a trip to Hollywood in 1956. Although he returned to Canada, he ended up performing underage at a night-club in Gloucester, Massachusetts until he won the first prize of a trip to New York in a contest which involved saving soup-can labels. While there, he auditioned *Diana*, a song about a girl he knew, for ABC. Soon it was a number one hit.

Most of Anka's hit songs were his own compositions during the period of the late 1950s and early 1960s, among them *You Are My Destiny, Crazy Love, Lonely Boy, Hello Young Lovers*, and two to express his romantic relationship with Annette Funicello, *Put Your Head On My Shoulder* and *Puppy Love*. After a period of writing and recording in French, German, and Italian, as well as some acting roles in movies for which he sometimes wrote some of the music, he returned to the charts in the 1970s with another hit, *Having My Baby*, which, to no one's surprise, generated the wrath of thousands of feminists. More than 400 of his compositions have been recorded by the likes of Buddy Holly, Frank Sinatra, and Tom Jones. He has been extremely successful performing in Las Vegas ever since.

Beyond the obvious fact that both Anka and Morissette hail from Ottawa, there are a number of other comparisons, though their eras are in direct contrast. Among those comparisons are their songwriting prowess, their powerful initial success, the fact they moved away from Ottawa to continue their careers, and the fact that Ottawa has demonstrated, in some circumstances, its unwillingness to forgive the necessary exodus. There is no indication, at least beyond Anka's lyrics to *My Way*, to indicate that Ottawa or Canada was a force in his musical subject matter or success. But those were different times, and although the aforementioned political-economic trends of the 1990s have roots in Anka's era, if not before, the sense of disenfranchisement by his fans was not so pronounced as it is with Morissette's. Nonetheless, it's important to note that Ottawa, as a factor in the development of a musical artist, has a precedent function which, in these outspoken times of disenchantment, finds its form in Alanis Morissette. It is in Ottawa that she first had to notice the political structure of the times, grew up with peers disenfranchised by that structure, and first learned that Ottawa and, perhaps Canada as well, does not always appreciate its superstar upstarts.

"Ottawa had a front row seat to this star in the making," wrote Abraham and Provencher. "She sang *O Canada* at Riders [Ottawa Roughriders football team] games, hosted Winterlude and was the featured diva on CHEO telethons [hosted by Max Keeping]. Yet many locals are anything but proud of the evolution they've witnessed. They call her contrived, rejecting the prickly, alternative image that's brought her international fame. But it hardly matters. Alanis does not belong to Ottawa any more."

And Morissette's remarks at the Junos less than two weeks after these words appeared in print, while she stood at the podium clutching one of her five awards, seemed to at least acknowledge the truth of this remarkable paradox, that while Ottawa might reject the change that's come over her, she will at least appear to be gracious about her country in return. Which is why what she said bears repeating: "I just wanna say that most people's growth is done in private, an artist's growth is done in public. And I thank Canada, the country, for accepting that in me."

By now the historic details have been well reported. Alanis Nadinia Morissette and her twin brother, Wade, were born June 1, 1974, the youngest children of Alan and Georgia Morissette, described as a devout Catholic couple. There is another son in the family, Chad, who was three at the time of Alanis' birth. Alanis' father is a native of Ottawa, a teacher who eventually became principal of Our Lady of Fatima elementary school. It is reported that he was a football player, playing half-back for St. Patrick's football team. His wife, the former Georgia Feuerstein, also a teacher, came to Canada during Hungary's anti-Communist revolt in 1956. It is popularly maintained that Morissette's parents first met on a playground as children, and that her father approached her mother and told her at that time that he intended to marry her. Regardless, reports of the family's closeness prevail, especially where Alanis and her twin brother Wade is concerned. Although both brothers sing back-up on her first self-titled album ALANIS, Wade is the brother mentioned in most of her concerts — "he rocks," she says — and it is Wade who is the subject of her unreleased song *No Pressure Over Cappuccino* often performed in concert.

It is reported as well that Morissette's startlingly early ambitions to become a singing star were encouraged by her parents and, in interviews, she continues to describe them as very understanding about what she is trying to achieve, the lyrics to *Perfect* on JAGGED LITTLE PILL notwithstanding. Her mother, in particular, was fairly ambitious, not only about encouraging her, but in guiding the early stages of her career, more or less as a manager. By the time the Morissette's travelled to Lahr, Germany for a few years so that they could teach the children of military personnel there when Alanis was very young, it is admitted she talked about being famous one day even then. "People who know her say she never seemed like a kid," Abraham and Provencher comment. "Acquaintances call her an old soul." They maintain, at the same time, however, that Alan and Georgia Morissette worked hard to keep the family close. "Each night they gathered in the living room where each had to talk about something that had made them happy that day. They have always fended off suggestions they were pushy stage parents. 'I'm here to encourage her and support her, but not to push,' Georgia said in 1987. In the early days, Georgia, a strong-willed woman, acted as her daughter's unofficial agent, believing stardom was just an opportunity away. She could turn any chance meeting into a chance for Alanis." Abraham and Provencher also noted that the entire Morissette family has a streak of over achievement about it. "Chad, now married and living in Toronto, was an entrepreneur before he could vote. Wade, now travelling in Asia and songwriting, was not just an athlete, but a triathlete."

Morissette, while maintaining her parents never pushed her into show business, says so with some qualification. "I don't think there's such a thing as a dysfunction-free family," she told *Rolling Stone*. "My parents, I love them, I'd jump in front of a truck for them, but no matter what family you're in, there are going to be obstacles, and I'd be lying if I said there weren't any." Was there a push for perfection? "I just wanted to do whatever it took to get the approval of my parents and the people I was working with at the time."

It is perhaps a little ironic that Morissette's first inclination to perform for her family occurred when she was only three years old, after she saw the musical *Grease* with John Travolta and Olivia Newton-John. Now, in the 1990s, should Travolta and Morissette ever meet, Travolta is the perfect candidate to outline cautiously the fickle nature of superstardom. It wasn't long after *Grease* that his star waned for two decades before beginning to shine brightly once more not long before the release of JAGGED LITTLE PILL. But perhaps the conversation will be unnecessary. Morissette is such a poised and direct person, it is possible she has already addressed the fickle nature of places, audiences, and times, that she has come to grips with the waxing and waning appreciation of their cultural heroes most audiences demonstrate.

At any rate, after the performance of *Grease* she shortly memorized the words to every song. "Georgia Morissette knew then her daughter was no ordinary 'cutsie'," said Abraham and Provencher. No wonder both parents encouraged her to pursue the musical direction in which she precociously aimed herself. By the time she was six, she was taking piano lessons and, by the time she was seven, she was pursuing dance as well. By the time she turned nine she had taken to writing her own songs and, at 10, was appearing on CJOH's popular children's show, *You Can't Do That On Television,* still in syndication in the United States on the Nickelodeon network. "Like Madonna, the blonde ambitious CEO of her Maverick record label, Morissette invented her destiny with relentless drive, calculation and a healthy dose of luck."

Max Keeping claims he was enamored with her from the very beginning when he met her at the CJOH studios on Merivale Road in Ottawa. "She was so determined and so confident that she would make it." In most interviews, Morissette approaches this early television work with a sense of humor, remarking on mail she used to get from jealous fans upset by the fact that she was the pretty girl being wooed by two boys at the same time, a character later abandoned in favor of a more wholesome alternative. And there have also been reports that management would like to see the show disappear, in view of her new angry and direct image, but most of these are speculative. Regardless of whether or not the show's potential for negatively demonstrating Morissette's drive to be a performer is a valid concern, it did provide her with a disconcerting poise and confidence that would serve her well in the future, when, a few years later, she was being transformed into a dance music star in Canada. It also provided, by the way, a hefty allowance which she was able to save up until she could cut her first record when she was only 11 years old.

You Can't Do That On Television now enjoys a large cult following because of Morissette's brief stint on the program. She appeared on the show in 1986, after winning a talent contest which aired on CJOH. As mentioned, her role was that of the new girl all the guys wanted to date, but gradually her part was redefined into that of an average young woman. Among the cast during that period were Matthew Godfrey, Vikram Sahay, Amyas Godfrey, and Rekha Shah. Despite the success the program enjoyed in syndication with *Nickelodeon* in the United States, Morissette was the only cast member to not resume a more or less normal life after production of the program ceased by 1988. Some did, however, continue on with acting while others continued on with their post-secondary education.

"It was a good, stupid, sarcastic kind of show," Morissette told *Rolling Stone* in November of 1995. "Very obnoxious and very tongue in cheek." *MTV News* aired footage of a virtually unrecognizably young Morissette being slimed by her co-stars on the show. "At that time, jealous viewers wanted to slime Morissette too," said *Rolling Stone* writer David Wild, referring to her role as the girlfriend of the two male leads. "She went on to other acting work, including a 'horrible' movie in which she appeared as a rock singer named Alanis, and future *Friends* star Matt LeBlanc played her boyfriend."

But, as she told Wild, "music has always been my priority." According to Abraham and Provencher, Morissette's parents set up an independent record label, Lamor Records, and sent her to Toronto to work with keyboardist Lindsay Morgan, a friend, and then Rich Dodson, a former member of the Canadian rock group The Stampeders. The result was three singles, including 2,000 copies of Morissette's first song about being a jilted lover, *Fate*

Stay With Me. However, as Kenneth Gorman, a singer-songwriter who teaches English at Immaculata High School in Ottawa, recalls it during a story he wrote for Southam Newspapers, which appeared in *The Kingston Whig-Standard,* November 30, 1996, the copy she signed for him when she was 12 had only two songs, *Fate Stay With Me* and *Find The Right Man*. But she did go to extreme measures to sell the record herself.

What makes Gorman's piece so interesting is not just the personal reminiscences about a young woman who was already committed to musical stardom when he knew her and who asked him to keep an eye on her progress, but that it focuses on the Hyde Park Concert in London she performed in 1996, the first there in more than 20 years. It is a coincidence made all the richer by the fact Gorman, a Canadian tourist at the time, was in attendance at the 1975 Hyde Park concert, held May 31, featuring Don McLean. Ironic that he would get to know Morissette personally 11 years later, only to celebrate another 10 years afterwards her arrival on the same Hyde Park stage, as he puts it, "to represent the next generation of rock as the legendary Dylan, Townshend (Pete and The Who) and Clapton take their twilight bows."

According to Gorman, "I first met Alanis when we were participants in a talent show organized by the drama teacher at Immaculata High School in Ottawa in the fall of 1986. I was a teacher at the school, a singing, guitar-strumming, '60s-generation English teacher. For the show, I had put together a small band with two students. We were known by the strikingly inventive name Live Band. During the first rehearsal, I was pacing around the darkened auditorium awaiting our turn when my attention was arrested by the sound of a lovely female singing voice. Professionally produced music accompanied the singer. I turned to see a young girl in the spotlight on stage. She wore a baggy sweatshirt, jeans rolled up at the ankles and white sneakers. With her right hand she held a microphone close to her mouth. With her left hand, she swung the microphone cord to the rhythm of the music. Other than a little bounce in her legs, she moved very little from her spot at centre stage. She sang so well that I stood still for a moment, transfixed."

Gorman then approached the drama teacher to ask about the young girl and he was told not only that she was only twelve, but that the song was her own composition and that the backup music had been recorded in Toronto. "Just then, Alanis hit a high, powerful note but didn't move the microphone away from her mouth. I covered my ears. Before the end of the song, she hit that same note a few more times with the same painful effect. When she was through, I introduced myself and suggested that, for the sake of her audience, she should move the microphone away from her mouth on the strong notes and bring it closer for the soft ones." According to Gorman, she agreed to give it a try.

He reports that their first opportunity to sing together arrived when the school band required a filler between sets. "The music teacher asked me if I would be willing to sing a song. I consented, seeing it as a chance to sing with the wonderful new girl. Alanis agreed to join me and we settled on Elvis Presley's *Can't Help Falling In Love* as our song. We would do it *a la* Corey Hart. The plan was that I would sing the first verse and chorus while Alanis harmonized, then she would sing lead for the remainder of the song with my harmony. She had an excellent ear for harmony and, during practices, made up her own harmonies on the spot. Unfortunately, we found that our voice ranges were such that we couldn't find a common key for the solos. For the song to work, we would have to change from the key of G to the key of B flat in the middle of the song.

"When we rehearsed in a small room, the dramatic key change worked reasonably well, but I was hesitant to try it on stage in front of the whole school in case she couldn't find the B flat note, prompted only by a strum from my acoustic guitar. But Alanis had no such qualms. 'Let's give it a try,' she said. So there we were on stage in front of 700 people, too late to back out. I put on my teacher-knows-what-he's-doing face, but my palms were sweating. I feared I might drop my guitar pick. Alanis was relaxed and smiling. Not yet a teenager, she already had the poise of a veteran performer. We sailed smoothly through my solo. Then came the change of key. I strummed the B flat, which I was certain she could barely hear, nodded to her and held my breath. If she got off on the wrong note, we were sunk. Without missing a beat and exactly on key, Alanis began her solo. To this day, I don't know how she found that note, but I remember thinking to myself, 'This kid is good!'."

Gorman says she burst into his classroom one day to sell him her record, explaining that she had been selling them on the bus, to a woman who sat beside her. "I laughed and shook my head at the thought of a 12-year-old selling her own records on a city bus while on her way to school. But Alanis did not consider her behavior eccentric. She saw herself as merely taking the first steps down a path that would eventually lead to superstardom as a singer-songwriter. Such an outcome was not a mere possibility or even a probability. In her mind, it was a certainty."

The record jacket displays a mature looking Morissette, hair piled high, looking somewhat older than 12 years of age. "Dear Mr. Gorman," the jacket says, "Just think you've taught me all I know, and I'll never swallow gum again."

"Alanismania," Gorman reports, "has arrived, as the precocious 12-year-old said it would. I open my 1986-87 yearbook once again and reread her 'Hey, Mr. G.' note. Alanis has drawn an arrow from her signature to her picture on the page. The note ends with the words, 'Watch 4 me. Love, Alanis.'"

ALANIS
FATE
STAY
WITH
ME
you've taught me all I know.
and I'll never swallow gum again.

·two·

Forgiven

Oh, man, I wish I had me to listen to when I was 14.

— *Alanis Morissette*

You know how us Catholic girls can be
We make up for so much time a little too late
I never forgot it, confusing as it was
No fun with no guilt feelings

—*Forgiven*

The trouble with enjoying success, the extraordinary kind that Alanis Morissette has enjoyed with JAGGED LITTLE PILL, is that it distorts, within a crowded exaggeration, the typically pompous but rather apparent accuracy hindsight bestows upon itself when it pops in on us for a reflective visit. Hindsight, you see, is always right, or, as the old adage goes, 20-20. For most of us who partake of the analysis hindsight is wont to present, the process takes place in private — or in some boozy state of temporary intimacy with a friend willing to listen. And if we succumb to hindsight's stubborn assertion that it is invariably accurate, never mind whether it truly is or not, we usually emerge feeling unscathed, still fully clothed against an unkind world, our dignity and privacy intact.

For people like Alanis Morissette, however, hindsight is a different kind of ordeal because it takes place in a crowded gallery. It's like discovering millions of flies clustered on the walls of your living room where you're pensively sipping a drink and coming to grips with why you did what you did and who you were trying to impress when you did it. And every time you come up with a comfortable conclusion, the flies begin to buzz like a crowd of onlookers at a tragic accident, passing on the information from one to another until the buzzing gets so loud you can't hear clearly any longer the thought which seemed initially full of clarity.

It's obvious, in the candor of her interviews, the things she has said while standing at a podium, that Morissette has wanted to achieve this kind of success from a very young age. It's also clear that she considers the various musical directions her career took on the way to her JAGGED LITTLE PILL summit a creative, psychological, and emotional learning experience, a kind of artistic apprenticeship. She was very young, she was anxious to please, she wanted success, and she did the things she had to do to generate that success. The trouble is, however, all those flies just keep on buzzing. Somehow the woman who belts out her outrage in the lyrics of the songs on JAGGED LITTLE PILL is supposed to have felt a similar outrage as a very young child, to justify its credence now. If not, the whole enterprise is perceived as contrived. But the alternative seems rather ridiculous, especially if one playfully imagines a three-year old Alanis performing even a childish version of *You Oughta Know* for her parents in their living room, rather than the songs from the musical *Grease*. It seems likely such an incident would have ended her musical career then and there. Even Jesus of Nazareth didn't start teaching from the cradle.

And what should be obvious to anyone involved in the performing arts is that there is and always will be a marketing of any raw talent so that it reaches a potentially large audience. Just as there will be rain and war and influenza, there will be artists and *the marketing of artists*. If for no other reason than that they climb out of the seclusion of their basements so that we get to hear what they have to say. Without the marketing, we don't get to see the art. To equate the integrity of an artist with an unwillingness to be marketed or the non-existence of an apprenticeship in the craft is a dangerous over-simplification of the artistic process reaching its audience. It presupposes that popular acceptance of any kind of artistic endeavor automatically reduces its honesty and undermines its quality somehow. Worse yet, it tends to insult the audience. It maintains that if millions of people, deemed tasteless idiots for no other reason than their vast numbers, like an artist's work, it cannot be very good. It maintains, if millions are appreciating it, it must be contrived, else those same millions could never appreciate it. In virtually every art form on the planet, there is a clique which perceives popularism as a pariah. It is the founding cornerstone of every artistic club intent on keeping people *out,* the belief that what is appreciated by large numbers cannot be very good, else the great unwashed would not truly understand it.

In the period following the staggering success of JAGGED LITTLE PILL, Alanis Morissette has come up against these basic precepts which loiter backstage, intellectually effete thugs who cast a jaundiced eye at every artist's performance. And during this same period she has had to address countless times the early phase of her music career, her period of apprenticeship, her period of becoming an adult, and allegations, especially in Canada, of whether her most recent artistic direction reflects the integrity she claims it does.

"Morissette's early musical output is fairly generic," wrote David Wild in *Rolling Stone* in November of 1995. "Her pipes were already powerful, but the only quality that ties her first two albums to her current material is a healthy sense of adolescent lust. 'You're just a party, party, party boy / From the moment I walked into your life / I knew right then it was a serious thing for you,' she sings on *Party Boy* from 1991's ALANIS. Things took a darker turn on *Big Bad Love* from her 1992 follow-up effort, NOW IS THE TIME. 'I'm having dreams in the night of you, baby,' she sings, 'and Sigmund Freud would have thought I was crazy.'"

"No, I'm not scared people might hear those records," Morissette told Wild. "I never did *Playboy* centerfolds. There's nothing I regret. Maybe people will just understand my lyrics now a little more if they hear those records. It validates this record."

"Hey," interjects Wild, "unless you're Stevie Wonder or Michael Jackson, how would you like to listen to a record you did when you were sixteen? . . . She doesn't disavow the earlier recordings, but she considers JAGGED LITTLE PILL her 'real' debut."

"There was an element of me not being who I really was at the time," she told Wild. "It was because I wasn't prepared to open up that way. The focus for me then was entertaining people as opposed to sharing any revelations I had at the time. I had them, but I wasn't prepared to share." Morissette also spoke candidly about other differences between then and now, not only with regard to her music, but with respect to organized religion and the sexual repression it sometimes creates. While growing up she went to church every Sunday and attended a Roman Catholic school. "Then I rejected the whole concept of organized religion. Still do. But now when I'm on stage, it's very spiritual. I feel very close to God when I'm up there. . . . I was active and physically doing the things that were sexual when I was younger. There was one side of me that was crazy and deviant, doing things ahead of my time, and another side that was very held back, wanting to remain virginal for the sake of being the good white Catholic girl."

Wild reported that "these sorts of tensions" led the overachieving Morissette to a few episodes she describes as breakdowns.

"I had a few," she told him. "That sort of comes from a passive-aggressive approach. From the time I was ten, I was working with all these people trying to control me and tell me what they thought I should be and what I should look like. And I tried to control myself to be what they wanted me to be."

And these tensions indeed appear in the lyrics of her more "serious" songs on the first two albums, seeds for JAGGED LITTLE PILL. Take, for example, *Time Of Your Life* from NOW IS THE TIME:

Standing there on a road that leads to anywhere
Like a child left in the wilderness, standing there
penniless
Wanting to be the best . . .
Look at me, I'm a girl that some may preconceive
Why do they try to generalize, why are they
antagonizing me . . .

— *Time Of Your Life*

Or perhaps more graphically, if even more catchy, from *Oh Yeah!* on ALANIS:

My name is Alanis I'm just sixteen
So gimme a break I'm no disco queen
Just hear what I'm sayin' you don't wanna miss
I got a message 4 you and it goes like this

— *Oh Yeah!*

John Pareles of *The New York Times*, in a profile in February of 1996, reported that Morissette appeared barely older than "the high school girls who flock to her concerts," but that she is able to bring fresh memories of teenage betrayals and identity crises to her concerts.

"I didn't have high self-esteem when I was a teenager, as I think most teenagers don't," said Morissette. "I used to think I was alone in that. Oh, man, I wish I had me to listen to when I was 14."

Consequently she considered herself an entertainer more than an artist expressing herself. "My public musical performing self and then my personal intellectual communicative self were completely different. I spent so much time having the two worlds and keeping them separate, and I realized not only how frustrating that was but how unfulfilling that was." She carried this approach to youthful life into a string of bad romances. "I was always trying to please everyone. Not just boyfriends, but platonic friends, and producers, too. After the 20th bad relationship, I decided it wasn't just the men, it was something in me. I just got away from everything I had been trying to be for so long."

"When she left Canada for Los Angeles three years ago she was something of a mess," wrote Phil Sutcliffe in *Mojo Magazine*. "A zealously Catholic upbringing left her mixed up and repressed about sex and relationships. Adventures as a 10-year-old TV personality (in the sort of show that features a 'slime tank') and a 16-year-old pop star (two albums on MCA) had left her disillusioned. The consequence had been frequent and crippling anxiety attacks, fainting fits and crying jags."

"There are certain mistakes that you make when you're 16 because you're ignorant," she said during her well-known and controversial *Spin* interview in November, 1995. "No wonder she refers to JAGGED LITTLE PILL as 'my debut album,' and lowers her head in shame when referring to her two dance-oriented, teen-spirited chartbusters. Alanis was the Debbie Gibson of Canada," reported *Spin*.

"It was kind of a blessing that it was over," Morissette said, "because I wanted to start out with a clean slate, not only personally but career-wise, too. It left me sort of naked. Leaving Toronto to go to L.A. gave me a severe dose of disillusionment that was really necessary. I was finally in a position where things weren't working out. And it was good for me. It made me realize that certain people I'd blindly trusted let me down. My intuition was saying 'Don't trust these people, don't work with these people,' and I went against it."

"While the alternative rock world welcomes female artists," wrote Tom Moon prophetically in the *Houston Chronicle* in August that year, "in the larger pop world the stereotypes — tramp, high-minded singer-songwriter, dance-pop diva — still prevail at the top of the charts. Morissette wants to challenge that thinking."

"When I was 16, I would have said, 'Yeah, put me on the

cover.' But it's not about my cleavage, and I think people are a lot more open now to hearing what (women) have to say. And there are a lot more women being emotionally honest and naked about things than men are," said Morissette.

Back in Canada, however, where music pundits could still remember the first Alanis, there was a growing suspicion about her apparent evolution from pop diva to outspoken alternative artist. "Morissette's success in both the United States and Canada owes as much to canny marketing as it does to her singing and songwriting abilities," wrote Nicolas Jennings in *Maclean's*. "And the launch of JAGGED LITTLE PILL has been handled differently in each county. South of the border, where she signed with Maverick Records, the label owned by Madonna, Morissette is making her recording debut and has therefore been launched as a brand-new artist. Both Maverick and Morissette's Los Angeles-based manager, Scott Welch, have confidently aimed Morissette at fans of alternative rock — which includes such less commercial styles as grunge, thrash metal and neo-punk, and has everything to do with an anti-Establishment attitude. But in Canada, where Morissette had two previous, dance-pop albums, Maverick's distributor, Warner Music Canada, had to take a more cautious approach. Explains Steve Waxman, Warner's press and publicity manager: 'We knew that she might be up against prejudices because of her background as a dance artist. But we also knew that she had to answer for her past.'

"When Canadian media were sent advance copies of JAGGED LITTLE PILL, Warner withheld details about Morissette's background, hoping that critics would judge the album on its own merits. Perhaps the caution was not necessary, because even critics who were aware of Morissette's latter-day disco queen past were impressed by the new album. In fact, reviews across Canada were uniformly favorable. Meanwhile, Morissette's career as a teeny-bopper diva has not gone undetected in the United States. Both *Rolling Stone* and *Spin* picked up on it, with the latter referring to her Canadian albums, 1991's ALANIS and 1992's NOW IS THE TIME, as the singer's 'dirty little secrets.' For her part, Morissette, who has now begun turning down requests for interviews, denies being ashamed of the work."

Jennings homes in on the factor in Morissette's evolution which probably explains how a pop-diva could emerge a few years later with a confessional alternative like JAGGED LITTLE PILL, namely the longevity and persistence of her ambition to be a successful musical artist. "Josh Lovejoy," writes Jennings, "a friend at Glebe who sang with her in school theatrical productions, says that 'even though it might have been cheesy her wanting so badly to be a pop star, she was never embarrassed about it.'"

In another interview with Mark Brown of the *Edmonton Journal,* Morissette said, "The reason why I'm a lot more peaceful now, ironically, a lot more so than when I was younger and I had this (fame) on a smaller scale, was that when I was younger, my perception of all this was different. I was motivated by just thinking that if you had all this external success that everyone would love you and everything would be peaceful and wonderful. I found the opposite to be quite true, in fact. I saw music as a way to entertain people and take them away from their daily lives and put smiles on their faces, as opposed to what I see it being now, which is a way for me to actually communicate, and a way for me to tap into my subconscious. I didn't realize that I would be able to do that through music, for many reasons, including myself being my own saboteur and being in creative environments that were not conducive to my feeling free and unjudged." And Peter Howell of the *Toronto Star* reported that "while she acknowledged much growth in her songwriting and performing, she made no attempt to disassociate herself from her earlier career."

"In many ways, it went exactly where I wanted it to go," Alanis said with respect to her first album. "And the second record, the one I did just before this, to me was an evolution as a writer. Even though it wasn't accepted by the people as well, I liked it better for what it represented in my life. So everything so far has gone the way I wanted. I have absolutely no regrets of anything that I've done, because had I not gone through that, I'm not sure this record [JAGGED LITTLE PILL] would have come out."

Alanis Morissette was only 11 when she met the next primary figure in her evolution as a musical star, figure skater turned choreographer/producer Stephan Klovan. By that time she definitely had her sights on a singing career and musical success but, at such a young age, was still in the preliminary stages of her artistic development. Klovan's guidance was destined to take her closer to the top of the musical pinnacle, yet it would sow the seeds of the backlash over Morissette's perceived contrivance by the time JAGGED LITTLE PILL set the world on fire.

According to the *Ottawa Citizen*'s Carolyn Abraham and Norman Provencher, as well as the *Ottawa Sun*'s Paul Cantin, Klovan had been asked by the National Capital Commission, the government agency which oversees cultural events in Ottawa, to produce an entertainment extravaganza for the Festival of Spring, also known as the Tulip Festival, and it was with respect to this project that he first met Morissette. Abraham and Provencher report that Klovan was looking for a girl Bryan Adams could pull from the audience at an upcoming concert. Cantin maintains that Klovan had already completed his auditions for this event when he received a call from a woman who wanted him to consider her son and daughter. The woman was Georgia Morissette.

Klovan lived nearby the Morissettes and he went over to their home to audition Alanis and Wade. When he took them out onto the family terrace and asked them to perform a cartwheel, Alanis demurred about the request. "If you want to be in the show, honey you're gonna do a cartwheel. We sort of hit it off. She was like 12 going on 30. I found her very mature, you know?" Klovan told Cantin.

According to Klovan, "She sang this song called *Find The Right Man* . . . here's this *11-year-old* singing 'Gotta find the right man.' So I said to her, 'Alanis, that's quite a mature song for an 11-year-old girl to be singing, do you understand the words?' And she said, 'Understand them? I wrote them!' "

"Klovan made Alanis and Wade the stars of the show," the *Ottawa Citizen* reported. "Dalmy's store executives swooned when they saw their performance. They wanted those kids, that girl, to promote the new DalmysKids clothing stores in Canada. Alanis wrote the jingle and Klovan carted the singing twins to openings in Ontario and Quebec. They spent weekends in hotels, Klovan in one room, Alanis and Wade in another. Life-size pictures of Alanis and her brother stood in a dozen malls. Strangers stopped to ask, 'Hey, aren't you the DalmysKids?' Klovan became Alanis' manager and the two developed a deep, lasting friendship. They called each other 'pukoo.'"

Cantin maintains that it was more than simply the fact Klovan got along well with Morissette. Apparently he recognized something else in her potential. "I sensed something right off the bat," said Klovan. "There's sort of a sixth sense you have in the entertainment business. She definitely had a undefinable quality. I guess you could say star quality. I auditioned a lot of kids for that show and I've auditioned lots of performers over the years and very few stand out with that little whatever it is, and she definitely seemed to have it and obviously does have it. But she had it way back then."

After the Festival of Spring experience, Klovan began to search out opportunities for his young singer. "At that time, Debbie Gibson and Tiffany were really big items in the States and Alanis was in that age group, so we were targetting the same market in Canada. She was actually kind of a little bit stiff as a performer at first, as far as her dancing and so on, but she learned quickly. She was aiming . . . to be sort of a pop little princess and so on."

By the time Morissette was 15, Klovan went with her to New York to audition for *Star Search,* where, according to reports, she attended musicals and exclusive dance clubs — "where doormen invariably hand-picked her from the lineup for looking so good," according to Abraham and Provencher. Klovan introduced her to what he termed "Ottawa society" in 1988 by booking her as the entertainment for a black-tie gala at the Westin Hotel to celebrate Olympic silver medalist Elizabeth Manley's first television special. Klovan had produced the special. Alanis performed in a black-and-white polka-dot Anne Klein.

Klovan's most interesting gambit to provide Morissette with the exposure she required, however, was to have her perform the Canadian national anthem at high profile events. One of these included the World Cup Figure Skating show where an audience of about 10,000 people heard her live rocking rendition. Ultimately this would become a local trademark, and, in some circles, she is still known as "Miss O Canada."

According to Abraham and Provencher, Alanis approached her parents to announce that, while she and Klovan were having a good time, "he has taken me as far as he can and I need another step. Help me find another step." An assortment of coincidences connected her to musicians Leslie Howe and Louise Reny of One 2 One, and, over the next few years, this connection would indeed move her career a few steps further forward.

One 2 One had its roots in another group, Mainstream, which had performed covers of other hit artists during the period 1975 to 1983. However, by 1984 Howe and Reny were a duo who eventually signed with Bonarie Records, distributed by WEA Canada. Their debut album FORWARD YOUR EMOTIONS produced the single *There Was A Time* and then, in the United States, *Angel In My Pocket.* As early as 12 years of age, Alanis had tried to connect with One 2 One by approaching singer Reny after mass at St. Mary's Catholic Church. Reny, it is reported, was taken aback by "the gutsy kid," but had reservations about the impact of a musical career on someone so young.

"I just though she was too young, not that she wasn't good enough. I just thought, 'you should be having fun,'" she said, recalling having brunch with Alanis' mother Georgia, where, it was reported, Georgia did most of the talking. "I missed out on high school events and everything because I was playing in a band . . . so I thought, 'wow, 12? You don't want to join a band . . .'"

Morissette, of course, had another view of both her age and her music. "I want to prove to people that just because you're young, it doesn't mean you can't do as much as adults can," she said in a profile in *Ottawa Magazine* in 1987. Having already written the lyrics for about 30 songs, she said, "I just think of what people listen to and then I write it down . . . It's like poetry and stories together. You write down the words that rhyme."

But it almost seemed that destiny would connect Morissette with the principals of One 2 One. The other partner in the duo, Leslie Howe, had already been one of the collaborators on her World Figure Skating Championships performance of *O Canada* when Alanis' parents bumped into him at a local restaurant and

Georgia asked him to work with her daughter. By then, One 2 One had a second album and was in search of a new record deal. Howe was looking for additional work on the side for a studio the duo had created. He terms the point of their collaboration with Morissette, around 1988, as "a starting place."

"It wasn't like these songs are the greatest," he said about an early demo tape he heard of Morissette. "I saw some raw talent there and thought we could develop it. At her age, she was pretty advanced even back then. She had a great voice. She had a great personality. And I just sensed she's pretty cool for her age. . . . It's hard to explain, but when you work with somebody in the studio, you get a feel for their musical ability and creativity and she has just from the beginning been a talented girl. She has this charisma thing. I hate to use that word, because it is such an unquantifiable thing, but she just has this personality and this air about her, that she's just a likeable person. . . . I wasn't thinking: 'Hey, we're going to be millionaires and we're going to sell millions of records.' I don't know if anybody thinks like that. It was more like hey, this girl is good, she can sing good, she has talent, she's got a great personality and great looks. Perhaps we can do something together. I guess it's something I just happened into. It's not something I'm looking for and it's not something I set out to do. It just sort of fell into my lap and I wanted to explore it."

Klovan and Howe teamed up to prepare some material for Morissette to perform on *Star Search*, material which had to fit a rather strict series of requirements. Although original material is appropriate for the program, cover tunes must come from a catalogue of approved numbers. Among the other requirements, because of the television format, was that the performance be exactly one minute and 45 seconds long. In the end, one of the cover tunes she performed was *One Bad Apple*, previously recorded by the Osmonds.

"I like to write on my own," Howe said later. "I'm sort of embarrassed working out raw ideas in front of somebody. So I normally get some musical pieces together, and Alanis and I would work out melodies together and work on the lyrics. For the most part, I wrote lyrics for the first album."

It was a whirlwind time for the young Morissette. Not only was she in her first year at Glebe Collegiate, but often she would bicycle across town to Howe's studio, often on a daily basis, and sometimes she would stay as late as one a.m. At the same time, Klovan was helping to groom Morissette's look as well, with the help of clothing retailers who expressed an interest in sponsoring what was purported to be a promising young singer. Even her connection with Dalmy's continued as she modelled for one of their catalogues and appeared at some of the chain's stores.

Although she did her utmost to conceal it, Morissette later admitted she felt a great deal of pressure during that period of her life. "That whole teenage era, for me, I would not repeat for a million dollars," she said. "I'm glad I went through it and it contributed to what I am as a person for that I am grateful. But I would never want to go back to that time. And I hope one day I will be able to look back on it with some positive feelings, but right now, I can't. I don't have very many positive feelings about school in general."

For Morissette it was a matter of combining her age with her passion to be involved in the record and entertainment industries, "which sort of provides a certain amount of pressure and expectations that I steadfastly held on to and tried to rise to all the time. Any time you have that, you are going to be very disheartened. Nobody could ever live up to it all the time. But I was very much a perfectionist, over-achieving mindset. And anyone will tell you if you have that, you're going to be letting yourself down all the time. There were a lot of people depending on me, not just them looking good, but financially. I had people depending on me for their money. Their careers were based around me." As she would later sing in *Perfect* from JAGGED LITTLE PILL, "We'll love you just the way you are if you're perfect."

Although Morissette's parents were aware of these pressures, they didn't interfere. "In many ways, they felt their hands were tied," she said. "They knew that in order for me to get away from the pressure it would mean my getting out of the music industry. And they knew if they even suggested it, I would never agree. It was my decision. To this day I know that this is what goes along with it. If that's what I want to do, there are certain sacrifices. I know the public perception of who I was at the time came across as a confident person, and in many ways I was. And in many ways I wasn't and I almost denied most of that part. I just don't have very positive feelings about that era. I'm grateful for it and I wouldn't change it. But I wouldn't go back."

And so while Morissette was coming to grips with a level of pressure inappropriate to most young teenagers, the supporters in her corner, Stephan Klovan and Leslie Howe, were working on how best to obtain a recording contract. At last the pair came up with a unique approach. They decided to produce a slick video for the song *Walk Away,* which Louise Reny and another Ottawa musician, Frank Levin, had co-written for her. Nor were they going to go cheap, despite the fact they had no backing from a major label for the video. It was an outrageous proposal. They decided to film the video in Paris to make the most of Morissette being filmed in an exotic location.

According to Klovan, the video was designed as a promotional tool for all the record labels. Klovan as a promoter and image-maker liked the idea of Paris because it would give her an "international aura," not to mention the mystique of having been around a little bit. Howe, on the other hand, seconded the idea because it was the best way to demonstrate what Morissette had to offer, in view of her music being created with keyboards and computer-sequenced, programmed rhythms.

According to Abraham and Provencher, "Nailing down sponsorships from airlines and Hilton Hotels, Alanis flew to Paris for ten days to shoot the video with Howe, local director Dennis Beauchamp and Klovan. . . . The video is fast and flashy: Alanis dancing on a Paris sidewalk; spinning in floral prints by the Seine; splashing in a fountain by the Eiffel Tower and smiling. Always smiling. After work, they would hit the nightclubs and one night Alanis was invited to a party with Diana Ross and, even though they had a nice conversation, Klovan says she 'wasn't really fazed.' At the Paris Hilton, Alanis' crew kept running into Bob Hope, who was there filming a TV special. Hotel management, taking stock of the entertainment types in house, held a cocktail party for Hope and Alanis."

As Klovan recalls it, "I said, 'Alanis, do you realize how lucky you are . . . you're in that league.' She sort of seemed destined to be mingling with the (stars) even in her early stages." He added, "How many parents would have trusted their 14-year-old daughter with three grown men? I wouldn't advise it for everybody her age. But in her case she was certainly mature and worldly enough to adapt."

But more than that the video reflected a tremendous risk on the part of Howe and Klovan. Howe was already in debt for his recording studio equipment, but he had a great deal of faith in Morissette's talent. "Just in short-term credit cards, loans from my dad and stuff, say close to a $100,000," he admitted later. "Looking back, it was sort of foolhardy. I mean, I don't know if I would spend that much now. I could have lost everything." As for Klovan's help with sponsorships and other financial initiatives, he added, "We were able to beg, borrow and steal. . . . We would try to use every possible way, so it would look like a lot of money was spent, without spending a lot of money. It's tricky but you have to be resourceful in this day and age. . . . It was one of those things where it all sort of fell into place."

More importantly, in the end, it was the video that earned Morissette her recording contract with MCA. Howe convinced Canadian A & R man John Alexander, a former member of the Ottawa band Octavian, to take a look at the finished product shot in Paris. According to Howe, "He flipped out. And we signed."

Alanis appearing with her brother Wade as a DalmyKid (top right), and being "slimed" on You Can't Do That On Television *(bottom left).*

·three·

All I Really Want

When it came time to think about an image, all I said is that I didn't want to be a fake. And it's really great because we wound up with me.

— *Alanis Morissette*

And all I really want is some patience
A way to calm the angry voice
And all I really want is deliverance

— *All I Really Want*

If anyone is keeping track of its history, rock 'n' roll is more than 40 years old. The trouble is, when you're that old, people tend to take you for granted. You take on that aspect of having always been around. You may have gone through a wide assortment of changes, but over all you're pretty old stuff. Sort of like a favorite shirt that's faded and ripped, been mended, tattered itself again, then been patched and worn one more time. An institution, really. Practically as old as music itself, though, of course, you know *that's* not really true. Regardless, the key byproduct of possessing such a long tradition is that you've been absorbed into the mainstream of human reality. You're not a distinct alternative anymore. You're not the voice of rebellion, for instance. Even to your detractors, you can't quite escape the inherent patronization behind your being pulled into the hesitantly changing human embrace.

In a general sense, the same rock 'n' roll which never wanted acceptance keeps receiving that acceptance anyway. No matter which direction it sets out upon, it keeps getting swallowed up by the mainstream. That's at the core of the irony which people perceive in change these days. If you want to diffuse the power of a firecracker, just insert it inside a stick of dynamite, which is exactly what the human condition keeps doing to rock 'n' roll. In the blast's aftermath, rebellion has been vaporized. All that's left is the same old status quo.

The main difference between the people of the sixties and the people of the nineties is that the people of the sixties didn't understand irony, or if they did, they were going to go on despite it. It was what made a popular idealism of their quest for change. The people of the nineties, however, have so honed their knowledge of this irony that they've tried to make the irony the rebellion itself. Which reflects a peculiar kind of self-devouring cynicism. There's a solidarity in group idealism because everyone keeps talking about the alternative, sharing the excitement of its possible achievement. But there's a loneliness in group cynicism because the only alternative is acceptance of the cynicism itself. At first, you can embrace a smug triumph in the fact that you privately know everything is a lie, that you, more than the idealist, are a realist. But sooner or later, too wise to believe the unbelievable, you have to deal with the fact that being a realist is just cynicism and being a cynic is just rationalizing the lack of integrity with which you blindly bind yourself to the status quo. In the end, all you can think of to do is get angry.

Rock 'n' roll is both at the root of and a mirror of such issues. It was born in a state of superficial rebellion, aimed more at the sensibilities of the status quo than at its truly basic evils. It was teenage angst, rebellion without a cause, perhaps its only legitimate aim to acknowledge the primordial jungle need we have to dance and drumbeat ourselves into a necessary, wanton frenzy made all the richer when so many disapprove of it. And perhaps to escape a societal repression of sex deemed so prerequisite to a structured civilization as to justify the denial of natural human need and pleasure. Society has rules. Rock 'n' roll, in its early days, set out to shatter those rules, but only the ones on the surface. Like burping without saying "excuse me."

Even with the British invasion of the early sixties, rock's rebellion was superficial. Long hair and weird duds. Until the idealism came along. Until a more focused rebellion came along. Until all that solidarity and shared alternative came along. Granted, it only took five minutes for the status quo to absorb, market, and trivialize that idealistic solidarity, but for that brief five minutes, it was truly there, it actually existed. Everyone was aware of what was "cool" then but it remained "cool," in the cocoon of that idealism just the same. By contrast, the age of irony is so cynical about what is cool, it's not cool the very instant after it's been deemed cool in the first place. And if there's any rebellion in standing on stage and spitting at your audience, it's disarmed by the cynicism which absorbs it into the mainstream, because there is no true movement or alternative behind it. If the mainstream of society transforms the rebel in most of us into a brief anger without alternative, by absorbing us into the mainstream, it does not accomplish this nearly so completely as does our cynical belief that it will inevitably do so.

The idea of rock 'n' roll was that it was anti-Establishment. By the sixties, more or less in response to the Establishment's attempt to make rock music Establishment, the genre split at a fork in the road. Even back then there was mainstream rock and alternative rock. Mainstream rock was society's disarming of rock itself. Alternative rock was the continued voice of the rebellion. This hasn't changed in the three decades since. Grunge, neo-punk, metal, and various other alternative presentations of rock are the modern reflection of that same rebellious split away from the mainstream pop venue that is society's version of what palatable rock should be like. There is, however, a major difference between the idealism of that sixties fork in the road and the cynical irony of what the alternative road has become in the nineties. When the sixties alternative was cool, everyone who got involved was cool. When the nineties alternative is cool, well, it isn't cool anymore. Which leaves everyone on their own, with their angst and their frustration over what the world has become, and with no alternative available. Because, as nineties people will quickly tell you, there is no alternative that isn't a lie.

There is a validity in the comparisons of Alanis Morissette to The Beatles beyond her meteoric rise to superstardom and the sales of JAGGED LITTLE PILL. It's in the route she has taken on her way to success, her approach to that fork in the road between mainstream and alternative rock. Morissette, like The Beatles, began her career on the mainstream branch, then later moved to the alternative branch. JAGGED LITTLE PILL's success, however, has *mainstreamed,* if you will, the alternative. Which means, in this age of irony, alternative music has to go somewhere else, for fear there will be a movement, that the movement will have an alternative or an ideal, for fear the integral cynicism in knowing that truth is just thousands of brilliant lies has been betrayed, that the battlements of non-belief have been breached.

Morissette embarked on her musical career with the idea that she was a musical commodity with the sole purpose of entertainment. When this direction did not satisfy her personal creative needs, she exorcised herself of her artistic demons. In so doing, quite inadvertently, she became a commodity again. If there is any dishonesty in this development it lies more with the mainstream than it ever could with her. Her generation of fans, with their entrenched sense of irony and their entrepreneurial spirit — the one lie they do believe is that the corporate club wants to give them a key to the executive washroom when, in fact, corporate clubs, like the artistic clubs, are created to keep people *out*, not let them in — runs the risk of being tempted to believe in a movement, the traditional rock movement of unabashed rebellion based on a reaction against dishonesty.

That's what the backlash against Alanis Morissette is all about. It's generated on two sides: by a mainstream which can diffuse the honesty by absorbing it, and by a generation of cynics who, seeing this absorption taking place, question the legitimacy of the very honesty itself.

"I laugh now," replied Morissette early last year when Jon Beam of the *Minneapolis-St. Paul Star Tribune* asked her what she makes of all the backlash. "There were moments when I wasn't laughing. If something's true, why are people so quick to doubt it? They've had the wool pulled over their eyes so often that they're compelled to throw the baby out with the bath water, simply because they've been snowed so often. I think the norm in the late '80s was to be something that you weren't. I fell directly into that category. It's hard for them to adjust to a decade where people are being themselves. And that goes beyond music."

But even if Morissette seemed to know what was going on, certainly seemed confident about her integrity in spite of all of the debate, from sensation to backlash and back again, the debate nonetheless went on. "Armed with a distinctly powerful and theatrical voice, as well as tunes that stick in your brain and ring with poignancy, Morissette has found a shtick that really works — pop-soluble anger," wrote Marisa Fox for *The New York Daily*. "That emotion colors every facet of her performance, from the way she twists her voice into wails and gasps, to the way she stretches words into pained vowel sounds, to the way she contorts her limbs into awkward knots, to her confessional songs about betrayal, rejection and lust. New teenage fodder this isn't, but Morissette's tortured tales found a deep resonance with the mostly college crowd who sold out the first of a three-night engagement in New York City. Though definitely not part of the grunge or alternative scene, the audience swayed, waved, moshed, ignited lighters, whistled, screamed and knew every lyric to her songs — even the men sang along.

"During an impassioned version of *Hand In My Pocket* the

crowd high-fived, made peace signs and waved on cue, further proof that this 12-year entertainment-biz veteran had her routine down pat. Morissette has not only cornered the market on young, disenchanted females who viewed her show as a mass-empowerment session, she also attracted men to Roseland who were, no doubt, piqued by this self-professed pervert who sings about performing oral sex in public places. But in the flesh, Morissette was no out-of-control Courtney Love. If anything, she appeared as an androgynous rock star in shapeless, baggy leather pants and a loose blouse, flailing the mane that hid her face. Ironically, her band, a poor Red Hot Chili Peppers soundalike (real Peppers Dave Navarro and Flea play on her album only), exuded the kind of machismo she rails against. Then again, maybe Morissette isn't quite the female malcontent she says she is. Her hormones rage only within safe pop parameters and her lyrics — full of "I don't want . . . I don't want . . . I need . . . I suffer . . . I'm tired . . . I hope" — betray the fact that she's more brat than bitch. Ultimately, this 21-year-old wants what most in her age group seek: acceptance."

Morissette's supporters, however, have difficulty understanding this controversy over her image. As reported in the *Ottawa Sun*, her manager, Scott Welch, questioned, "Why is everybody giving her such a hard time for work she did in her teens? It's as though you really resent the fact that she's trying to do something different now and won't allow her a scrap of credibility. . . . you go through a major change in your values, everything, from the time you are 16 to 21. You move out of the house, you realize everything your parents said wasn't true. People refuse to give her that space. None of us can know how we would react if you were 14 and suddenly you are a celebrity in Canada. I think the difference now is at 14, she's got the record company telling her to do something. You can't make all the right decisions. Now, she is making her own decisions."

Songwriting collaborator Glen Ballard was equally perturbed by the controversy, by allegations that the music he worked on with Morissette was canny marketing. "Oh God! Zero calculation in that respect," he said. "It was real, truly the most uncalculated thing that I have ever been involved with. There's no doubt it was a genuine and artistic awakening. If we had been calculated, we would have looked at what she had done before and said: How can we relate what we are doing now to what you did? I had never even heard that stuff (on her first two albums). I didn't know where we were going with it. We had hands on the Ouija board, man, and I'm telling you it took off. This is where it was supposed to be. The last thing we were trying to figure out was what we were supposed to do in terms of the marketplace. We were giving blood every time we sat down to do it. We don't know how to do it any other way. We were not on cruise control. We were really beating ourselves up every time."

Yet Morissette wasn't startled by the controversy. "Nothing has really surprised me," she said. "I knew people would have a little bit of trepidation towards what I was communicating now, compared to what I was prepared to communicate back then. And so far, a lot of people have been very open to it. Perhaps a little more open than I thought they would be. It has been really great. It is really satisfying to be able to communicate this honesty now, and have people not only accept it, but understand it, and dive right in."

Even after the 1996 Grammy Awards, reporters, writers, and even musical superstars themselves were dragged into the debate about whether Morissette was what she is billed to be, whether she is something else and whether any true comparisons can be made. "The night's surprise winner for best pop album [Joni Mitchell] seemed to take offense when asked if she thought fellow Canadian Alanis Morissette had assumed Mitchell's self-confessional songwriting stance," wrote George Varga of the *San Diego Union-Tribune*, recounting Mitchell's response. "I was never self-confessional," said Mitchell. "My songs were more like Shakespearean soliloquies."

The issue seemed further complicated by media disapproval when Morissette began to turn down requests for interviews later in 1996. As reported in the *Ottawa Citizen*, all calls for interviews are now referred to Mitch Schneider, a San Bernadino publicist who maintains that the silence is not image control but part of an "organic process to preserve the integrity of (her) career. The dangers of overexposure are huge. It's a disposable society and attention spans can be terribly short."

Still, as the momentum behind JAGGED LITTLE PILL increased and as Morissette continued to disarm her critics with honest answers, the music world came to see her as the real thing, not the "Miss Thing" of her song *Right Through You.* "For all the talk of her being the 'angry young woman' of rock 'n' roll, Alanis Morissette on Saturday acted more like a reborn hippie than a barb-throwing cynic," reported the *Boston Globe*. "She was never aloof, which some 'angry' singers take as their trademark. . . . Her message was one of release and healing, not of hatred or despair. She has transcended her romantic bitterness — and that was a valuable lesson to impart to this young crowd, whose female fans, especially, sang along as though this were group therapy."

Mark LePage of the *Montreal Gazette* was more than willing to give Alanis the benefit of the doubt, especially in the context of a comparison with rock singer Courtney Love. "While the media were lauding Courtney Love as the uncontrollable yin storming rock's yang primacy, the industry was sitting up and taking notice of the Canadian girl breezing past her to the spokeswoman podium," he said. "And since it was her critics who first raised unflattering comparisons between the purportedly phony Morissette and the achingly real Courtney Love, only a fool would fail to pick up the argument and flip it over.

"Morissette's past holds no harbingers of what was to come. She started professional life as a prefab teen dance-droid, a Canadian Debbie Gibson. Autopsies on her two albums reveal only a vocal similarity. The bite, then, is somewhat there. But the bark? Nothing in the *Plastic* single foretold a breakthrough breakup single whose heroine, a vengeful jiltee, recalls oral assignations in the cinema. And swiftly, we were hearing the flipside, about the men who 'took a long hard look at my ass / and then played golf for a while.' On the surface, she would seem to have everything in common with Love: anger, self-assertion, the risque language. Morissette's critics charge her with calculated raunchiness, which implies, we assume, that her doppelganger is the soul of sincerity."

LePage pointed out, however, that JAGGED LITTLE PILL also has a classic pop strength, not to mention the apparent self-assurance of its performer. "But what resonated just as deeply was the respectability, even the healthiness of the persona behind the hooks. Morissette is sexy by default, sexy because she deals with sex and not because she pouts or shows cleavage or affects the kinderwhore look. There is nothing empoweringly slutty about her. If anything, her onstage dress, in rumpled leather pants, is casual to the point of androgyny. Audiences don't feel threatened, nor that they are being sold anything. When Morissette sings about broken relationships and bristles at objectification, she does so exuding stability. Morissette sounds like she's done some hard thinking, found a talented male partner to refine her pop smarts, and addressed whatever demonettes there are in the closet and the diaries."

He was not so sure about Courtney Love. "Love sounds like she fell off the couch in mid-barbiturate binge. JAGGED LITTLE PILL presents the risque in an almost therapeutic context, by the woman least likely to take her clothes off mid-song, or need a methadone shot in the delivery room. There is no danger here, and no punishment either. It's Oprah, not Penthouse . . . . Calculation isn't necessarily the issue; palatability is. Perhaps that means the world isn't ready for Courtney Love's rawer sensibility, but it hardly means Morissette's is a soulless PR coup."

Even *Time Magazine* took a benefit of the doubt stance when Christopher John Farley wrote about the contrasts between JAGGED LITTLE PILL and Morissette's earlier albums. "The sound is more muscular, her voice is rawer, the guitar work more aggressive. The songs are about such topics as postbreakup rage (*You Oughta Know*) and overbearing parents (*Perfect*), and while the words are rarely as smart as they seem to think they are, this is straight-ahead rock, sweetened somewhat with pop melodiousness. But it is the transformation of Morissette's persona that makes JAGGED LITTLE PILL so intriguing. Rebellion — against society, against one's past — is, after all, the essence of rock. When, on *Right Through You*, she sings, 'You took me for a joke / You took me for a child / You took a long hard look at my ass / And then played golf for a while,' it's as startling as Chelsea Clinton with a Mohawk. Morissette's anguished, sometimes screechy voice is the sound of postadolescent independence. She's in the driver's seat now."

It's true that there has been a kind of acceleration of maturity in Alanis Morissette's life, beginning with the precociously early age at which she seriously contemplated a musical career, and it's a maturity which conveys itself now in her concerts, interviews, and media appearances, despite the fact she is barely into her twenties. Even before the recording contract with MCA which resulted in her first two Canadian albums, early career collaborators like Stephan Klovan and Leslie Howe found her maturity surprising. But the acceleration to the present was not always a smooth one. Along the way there were bumpy periods with men, creative and artistic traumas, and a deep self-examination into the nature of her personal goblins, many of them, she would say later, focusing on her Catholic upbringing. There were also periods she describes as breakdowns. Ultimately, analysis of these demons would accelerate the self-awareness she now presents when she performs, the assurance which is part of her enticement to so many fans. A self-professed reader of psychological self-help books, she has admitted to periods in her past when she sought to control people, alluded to co-dependence, and more directly referred to the battle between ego and super-ego most of us go through to varying degrees. The astonishing thing is that she appears to have worked out these powerful demons at a much younger age than many of us do.

Nonetheless, it isn't easy being a teenager and it wasn't easy for Alanis Morissette either.

"It hasn't been an overnight success by any means, although it may seem like that," Klovan told Paul Cantin of the *Ottawa Sun*. "She had a series of setbacks. It was very difficult for her going to school. And I know it was frustrating, you know how kids at school can be cruel . . . She always rose above it, but that part was frustrating. There's always a certain amount of rejection in this business you have to take. MCA wasn't the only label approached, and some of the other ones said: Don't-call-us-we'll-call-you type of thing. You have to step out of yourself as a performer and not be overly critical about rejection. It's not meant to be taken personally, but some performers do. But Alanis was pretty good about it."

Carolyn Abraham and Norman Provencher of the *Ottawa*

Citizen also report that there was some ambivalence on Morissette's part about her life in high school during this period. "At school Alanis was teased about her success but shrugged it off, continuing to juggle classes, recording and performing," they wrote. "She hung out with the fashionable, big-haired girls in frosted pink lipstick. She led a lunch-time aerobics class, sang at assemblies and, in Grade 12, she and Wade lip-synced to her favorite musical, Alanis as Newton-John, Wade as Travolta."

During high school, drama was her favorite subject and, since that period, Morissette has even hired her drama teacher, Jocelyn Rehaume, as her tour manager. She also had a special affection for English, but her Grade 9 English teacher, Bruce MacGregor, admits she did not distinguish herself in the subject. "She would leave and go on these wicked trips, two weeks at a time. It didn't help her marks, but there it was — she was cutting a record in L.A.," MacGregor told the *Citizen*. "Her first focus was her career and who could blame her?"

Music partner Leslie Howe was also aware of the pressures on Alanis to split her life between the more normal demands of school and her age group and the more unique requirements of focusing on a musical career. "She was always very cool about things," he said. "There were stressful times, for sure. It's not always, like, every day, things are fun and easy-going. But considering this was her growing-up period and going to school and juggling all the time needs to go to school and social life and doing the music career, she handled it extraordinarily well, as well as anybody could be expected to at that age."

Morissette, at the time, was also trying to garner performing experience, her reason for singing with a local cover band known as the New York Fries. In the end, succumbing to all the other pressures, she decided to give up the band. "She was trying to please too many people," said Klovan. "She was recording, I had her booked all over the place, not only singing the national anthem, but all sorts of events. And then she was performing with New York Fries, and she found she had to make a decision to be a little more selfish and not try to please so many people. Fortunately, when the record deal happened and MCA stepped in, they sort of controlled things a little more. They know how to protect their talent. And once she became famous, everybody and their mother wanted her for everything. Every charitable event wanted her to appear at this and that. You have to be selective. It's never that she didn't want to be selective. It's never that she didn't want to support things, but you can only do so much."

Southam Newspapers writer Peter Howell reported in the *Calgary Herald*, citing Timothy White, editor-in-chief of *Billboard* in New York, that Morissette suffered a nervous breakdown in 1991, at the height of her fame as a dance song performer. Apparently Morissette told White she "freaked out" in the living room of her Ottawa home, as her parents were preparing to leave on a business trip. "I'd taken too much on myself, and for once I dropped my facade of total assurance," said Morissette.

"That experience, her problems with men and other travails all turned into the songs of JAGGED LITTLE PILL," wrote Howell. "White first heard the album as a rough advance tape sent him last April (1995) from a product manager at Maverick Records, Morissette's label run by an earlier pop sensation, Madonna."

"The minute I heard her record, I thought, oh my God, this is about growing-up experiences. This is about a kid going through grief and weirdness in an adult world. It's not something about a woman lashing back against a man, because there's a lot of tenderness and sweetness on the record too," White said.

Klovan has not painted an entirely negative picture of the pressures on the young Morissette. In many interviews about Morissette now, cited often is her sense of humor. Klovan, in those early days, enjoyed her sense of humor, too. "People always used to wonder about the relationship Alanis and I had. Every time they saw us we were laughing a lot, like we had a secret. . . . One of the things we did to sort of amuse ourselves was, if we were in a city and we were watching TV or something, we'd turn the volume down and make up our own dialogue for the TV shows, or if it was a really bad movie. But we honestly always had a good time, enjoyed each other's company, travelled a lot together. We made the best of it, played a lot of practical jokes on each other. One time in Quebec City, she was singing at this big event . . . We were staying at the Chateau Frontenac, she got my shaving cream and emptied the can of it into the sheets in my bed. So when I got into my bed, it was shaving cream city."

During this period, Morissette was taken to see other major performers, including Janet Jackson and, ironically enough, Madonna, at SkyDome in Toronto, the woman whose record label would launch JAGGED LITTLE PILL a few years into the future. It was all part of the excitement during the period when MCA finally released her first album, ALANIS. Co-written by Howe, Ottawa songwriter Serge Cote, and Morissette herself, the album consisted of pop numbers, usually with a pronounced dance beat. To no one's surprise, the comparisons with dance artists Tiffany and Debbie Gibson were made virtually from the beginning. It is this material which seems to contrast so drastically with the songs on JAGGED LITTLE PILL. Her objectification as "pop princess" began at this point and still persists in some quarters, much to the chagrin of her current career handlers. But the chagrin on Morissette's part dates back to those early days when, even then, she spurned the label music pundits were trying to bestow on her. Although there were pop artists she respected at the time, performers like Whitney Houston — whom JAGGED LITTLE PILL would ultimately dethrone in the category of largest-selling debut album — and Canadian Celine Dion, Klovan maintains Tiffany and Debbie Gibson were considered as a guideline, not people Morissette should emulate.

"She never wanted to be a Tiffany or Debbie Gibson. . . . We never tried to emulate them, but they were so successful, we kind of used them for a guideline for what she was doing. If it is working down in the States, maybe it could work in Canada. That was our initial attack."

Not surprisingly, as a co-writer on the ALANIS project, Leslie Howe also rejected the comparison. "I've never seen Alanis as a teenybopper artist. Even back then, the Debbie Gibson stuff and Tiffany was wimpy . . . bubblegum girlie stuff." Morissette, he said, had "a very mature outlook on everything. I don't think we were that bubblegummy. I saw her as — how do you explain it — a more streety, mature type outlook and type of music. . . . I thought there was an element . . . another sphere to it that Debbie Gibson and Tiffany didn't have."

"People are already saying to me, 'So, you're the next Tiffany.'

Well, I'm not," she said after the release of her first album. "When it came time to think about an image, all I said is that I didn't want to be fake. And it's really great because we wound up with me. I wear what I want. I'm not turned into somebody else."

A close look at the lyrics of Morissette's first two albums tend to reinforce Howe's assessment that there was "another sphere to it." Even more importantly, they tend to make it less of a shock that she has moved to the searing directness of JAGGED LITTLE PILL. There is, indeed, indications in those early lyrics, first from her debut album ALANIS, then from its not so successful follow-up, NOW IS THE TIME, that Morissette would evolve into something else. It's as if the media cumulatively decided that an integral part of the story of JAGGED LITTLE PILL's success was a required contrasting of it with her two previous efforts.

Except for Morissette herself who has persistently suggested that there was an evolution going on throughout her career, that a kind of honesty and directness were there from the very beginning, most musical pundits tend to dismiss her earlier work as from another planet. Perhaps the pop danceability is in marked contrast, but the song lyrics have a tendency to reflect a less mature and less searing self-knowledge than the lyrics to the songs on JAGGED LITTLE PILL while, at the same time, serving notice that the seeds of JAGGED LITTLE PILL were already sown.

On My Own, from the original ALANIS album, for instance, demonstrates the same self-analysis which has matured and become more blunt on JAGGED LITTLE PILL.

> Why do I feel it's all up to me to see that
> everything's right and it's how it should be?
> Why don't they just leave me alone?
> I've got to prove I can
> Little girl with stars in her eyes
> They've got her all figured out
> and there's nowhere to hide
> Why can't they all see who I am?
> When will they understand?
>
> — *On My Own*

In *Real World*, from her second LP, she sings:

> We play the game with determination
> We don't give a damn 'bout our reputation, baby
> It's not a game, it's a revelation
> Step inside the real world.
>
> — *Real World*

A close look at her work from this period makes it difficult to dis-associate her efforts then from what she presented on JAGGED LITTLE PILL, notwithstanding the new maturity on the album which made her a superstar.

Even more ironic are some of the comments she made to the news media during that earlier period, remarks which more than hinted at a precocious self-knowledge and even a clairvoyance about the heavyhanded comparisons pundits would make about her earlier work. "However," wrote *Calgary Herald* writer James Muretich in July of 1991, "despite her video exposure for the single *Too Hot* and her album on the verge of hitting the top 40 selling recordings in the country, Alanis maintains a refreshing perspective on both herself and her music. She's open to criticism ('it's good for me'), quick to laugh and, well, charming. She also knows that teen sensations, male and female, haven't exactly been known for their staying power, artists like Tiffany rapidly becoming known as Tiffer the Stiffer."

"I know," admitted Morissette to Muretich. "Okay, um, first of all, I have no idea how things are going to go. The next album I release, people could go boo, hiss, hiss, this girl's like another Tiffany or whatever. But the way I look at it, no matter how old you are, people will like your next album if it's a kick-ass one. Trouble happens when people run dry and their second album isn't any good. That's when people turn to excuses like, oh, she was only 16 or 17 or whatever. But if you just stay yourself and keep coming up with good stuff, I don't see any reason why you'd die out."

Canadian Press writer Stephen Nicholls, in an article published in the *Winnipeg Free Press* in November of that same year, reported that Morissette was about to begin work on her second album. "She's set to start writing her second album, which will take a different direction," he said.

"It's going to have maybe a bit more of a harder edge. It's not going to be as dance (-oriented). But I say that now and if you put me in the studio tomorrow, I might write something completely different," Morissette said then.

Nicholls, recounting how the debut album had almost reached platinum status in Canada, 100,000 copies sold, and how her single *Too Hot* had hit number four on the charts, pointed out that Morissette's sights were set on the United States market even then. "Her image is fun-loving teen, but she shows grownup poise," said Nicholls. "Her speech, for example, doesn't have the common teenage inflection that makes every sentence go up at the end like a question."

In a return engagement with interviewer Muretich the following year, in a story bylined Barb Livingstone, Muretich commented that her second album was less bouncy, more serious.

"I myself, as a person, have changed the last couple of years and I wanted to reflect that," Morissette said, "though I didn't want it to be like the Alanis Diary. . . . It's hard not to think of how commercial you want to be but then I just don't want to keep writing all kinds of commercial songs and writing for radio and for other people." She also commented even then that she likes to read biographies and books about psychology — "I love psychology."

"What about the pep talk you give on the first page of the CD liner notes," asked Muretich, "the one that goes 'be gentle, strong, kiss, kissing is wonderful,' talks about not being perfect, being excellent and not giving up and then ends with the line: 'I believe in you?'"

"I just wanted to show people a little bit about where I'm coming from," replied Morissette. "Obviously that poem is a little idealistic. No one's like that, really. But like you said, it's like a pep talk to me. Like when I read it, I go, 'cool.' That's what I want to strive for."

Morissette, limited only by her age and her unwillingness at that stage to open herself up entirely, was already alluding to the anguish and issues which JAGGED LITTLE PILL would address a few years later.

In the aftermath of the release of ALANIS in 1991 and its more than satisfactory Canadian success, not to mention her first single *Too Hot*, Morissette took some time to outline to the news media, during a press conference that spring, the support of her parents and family, to acknowledge how she felt they had been a stabilizing influence on her.

"They were super-supportive, because I don't know how many parents would allow a daughter so young to fly like I did . . . My family is really tight. They trust me because we've had the best relationship since I was really young. We're friends and they understand how much I want this," said Morissette. At the same time, however, it is reported that she flirted with the idea of leaving school to enable her to work on music full-time but in the end she remained in class, no doubt acknowledging the influence of two parents who were both teachers.

Too Hot's success, however, only accelerated the acceleration that was already part of Morissette's life. Although there was a tremendous element of excitement about the success she was achieving, there were also residual difficulties she continually had to address. For example, she was mobbed once at an Ottawa shopping mall, was besieged by freshmen trying to get a glimpse of her at Glebe Collegiate, and even endured strangers ringing her doorbell at home, in search of her autograph. The video for *Too Hot* featured a chorus of topless male extras and Morissette grew concerned about an image which implied promiscuity. "Having a little sex thrown in there is okay, but there's no way I want people seeing me and saying, 'She's only 16? Oh, that little slut, what is she doing?'" said Morissette.

Klovan later reported that Morissette had to sort out the success-accompanying problems of newfound "friends" who materialized to share in her fame. "Everyone in Ottawa claimed they knew her, and it's funny how people come out of the woodwork after somebody is successful. Somebody as smart as Alanis can see right through it. She had friends who were true friends and there were others who wanted to be friends because she was Alanis the recording star. That all reflected on the frustrating time she had dating people . . . . She was so much more mature than most boys her age, so you don't really know what their real intentions would be. To go out with her because she was Alanis The Singer, or because they liked her. So that was always an ongoing problem."

Yet most observers at the time declare that Morissette clung to her own sense of herself and maintained what she still exudes, an incredible self-possession. Don Marcotte, who was able to study her character behind the scenes at CJOH Television in Ottawa during the filming of a documentary about her achievements, said, "You could have taken her to meet the queen and she would have known exactly how to act. And she would have gotten what she wanted out of it without acting like she was getting what she wanted."

"There was nobody else like her in Canada," said Klovan, "so she clicked into the right place at the right time. There was obviously a big void for a performer of her style and calibre. Because she was so personable on these promotional tours, everybody just fell in love with her, the radio people . . . were only too happy to promote the heck out of her. Nobody could have expected it. The album did so well initially. I don't think MCA even expected it to do quite that well."

MCA was on hand later that summer to surprise Morissette with the presentation of a gold album for ALANIS, signifying sales of 50,000 copies in Canada. The event took place during an Ottawa Rough Riders football team half-time show, which not only featured Morissette, but dancers flown in from Toronto for the celebration. Her star was, at that point, dramatically on the rise.

Alanis Morissette's first visit to Canada's Juno Awards on March 29, 1992 at the O'Keefe Centre in Toronto, although exciting for her, was in sharp contrast to her 1996 visit. In 1992 she was an up and comer in Canada. In 1996 she was a world superstar. While in 1996, Morissette was virtually the star attraction of the annual awards, both in front of the camera and behind the scenes, Canadian music attention was focused elsewhere in 1992. Coincidences abound, however. Tom Cochrane performed in 1992, collecting four Juno awards for his MAD, MAD WORLD album and his hit single *Life Is A Highway*. He also performed during the 1996 awards. In 1992, Cochrane surprised everyone with his win in the Single of the Year category, beating out Bryan

Adams' *(Everything I Do) I Do It For You.* Adams received three Junos, including a Special Achievement Award, which served to ameliorate a controversy over whether Adams was the victim of a music industry backlash against his remarks that Canadian content regulations foster mediocrity. By 1996, the only controversy at the Junos was the fact that Morissette had so capably taken so many Junos, despite some heady competition from rising country superstar Shania Twain.

In 1992, however, Morissette was safely on the outside of any potential controversies. Nominated for three awards, Single of the Year, Most Promising Female Vocalist, and Best Dance Record, she was the object of a media campaign in Ottawa to make her the home town favorite at the awards. A special postcard by Morissette from the Junos was published in the *Ottawa Sun.*

"Talk about nerves!" the postcard says. "It's Juno weekend and my dreams are coming true. After all the work, there's a chance I might just be rewarded with a Juno tonight — but no more talk about that, we don't want to jinx things, do we? They said this was a high-pressure time for nominees, and they weren't fooling. On Thursday, I spent a lot of time doing phone interviews with writers from across the country and wrapped it up with an hour on the air with one of TO's [Toronto's] top dance shows. But, that's just the beginning! Yesterday, things started to get really wild. I spent some time taking in the seminars at *The Record* conference which brings together music retailers, musicians, entertainment professions (lawyers, agents and managers), and music journalists. Everybody talks shop, so I just figured I'd check it out and maybe pick up a tip or two. In the middle of that we dashed around the city — putting in appearances at MuchMusic and Electric Circus.

"And last night I got to have a little fun at Rock 'n' Bowl — the industry's big celebrity challenge out in Scarborough. But we had to cut the fun short, because this morning I was up bright and early and locked into a pretty heavy schedule, with the bulk of it devoted to rehearsing for the big show tonight. In fact, rehearsal starts at nine a.m. Then it's back to the hotel to change into my special Juno outfit. I know for a fact that no other girl will be wearing it, because I helped design the outfit with a friend

— so I think I'm safe from copycats. It looks like we'll be busy all afternoon. There's a pre-show bash at the O'Keefe Centre, a meet-the-nominees reception and another pre-show function where they'll hand out a lot of the Junos which aren't presented on the show. Some of my categories fall into this area, so I'll be nervous all afternoon."

Of the three awards for which she was nominated, Morissette captured only Most Promising Female Vocalist, but visibly excited she confessed to the audience that she had been dreaming about this day since she was a child. "The amount of time I spent waiting in anticipation of what was going to happen was just insane. Since I was nine years old I wanted what I have now," she said.

Klovan, who was in Toronto for the awards ceremony, later maintained that Morissette was surprised at the award. "That was definitely the icing on the cake for Alanis," he said. "It was very exciting. . . . I wasn't that surprised, to be honest with you. I just knew she was going to win. Don't ask me what it was. It just seemed to make sense. It was an acknowledgment. I don't know if Alanis was convinced. It seemed too good to be true for her."

Images of Alanis, c. 1992, from MCA records.

·four·

You Learn

I don't think I'm the kind of artist who comes across as "I'm a star, you can idolize me." I come across as "I'm human, you can relate to me." I'm saying what a lot of people would want to say but would be far too embarrassed to say it. I had been embarrassed to say it. I wrote from a very dysfunctional part of my subconscious that I rarely indulge.

— *Alanis Morissette*

You live you learn
You love you learn
You cry you learn
You lose you learn
You bleed you learn
You scream you learn

— *You Learn*

One of the most intriguing ironies about rock music is the tendency of music critics to dismiss the work as self-indulgent. To allege self-indulgence in rock music is akin to accusing the musical bar of having notes. All arts have a powerful component of self-indulgence. That's how the process works. The artist is compelled to examine self in the context of a large and powerful world environment, creates from this lonely self and resists that powerful world's requirement of conformity (to superficial selflessness) until the art is presented to the audience for its self-indulgent self-application. The artist becomes successful when the audience, denied self-indulgence in its daily affairs, reaches out to the work of art and vicariously receives a few safe moments of the same self-indulgence we all require, transmitted by the artist. It's the self-indulgence of the artist with which all audiences relate. They hear in words or song lyrics or even see on a canvas something they would have said themselves, something they have felt themselves, something they have seen in a powerful moment of perceptive self-indulgence they have not had the courage to share with an otherwise preoccupied world.

Notwithstanding that all art, all creativity, is self-indulgent, there is a kind of sophistication surrounding certain kinds of art. The sophistication revolves around the degree of self-indulgence perceived in the work of art. The more apparent this self-indulgence, the more superficial and limited is the work of art deemed to be. Without subtlety, critics like to say. Proper society has a kind of protestant and tyrannical view of self-indulgence. If one has to endure it in society, one may as well be exposed to it only in the works of society's eccentric artists, but, by God, it had better not appear to be the self-indulgence it actually is. It's sort of like sex. Everyone knows it's out there, but you don't walk up to people and casually mention you had sex last night, the way you might say you enjoyed a piece of chocolate cake.

Which brings us to rock music. Bearing in mind that rock music has always set out to kick conventional society in the shins, the characteristic of self-indulgence in rock has always been more obvious than it is in most other art forms. It's part of the rebellion. If conventional society doesn't want to talk about sex, rock music will. If conventional society is not truly open to political alternatives, rock music will ram the alternative down its throat. Finally, if conventional society finds self-indulgence tawdry, then rock music will be as self-indulgent as it possibly can be. Most artistic genres permit self-indulgence to some degree, perhaps in acknowledgment of its essential role in transmitting art to its audience through shared experience. Rock music, however, not only permits it, it actually has traditionally encouraged it.

As mentioned, one of the reasons for this is the inherent rebelliousness in rock music. Young people, to whom alternative rock traditionally appeals, are *hormonally*, if you will, self-indulgent, just as they are *hormonally*, if you will, rebellious. Their parents, on the other hand, are trying to run an orderly society here and have some notion that it just isn't proper to be either rebellious or self-indulgent. Generally speaking, it's a point of view they've adopted as they grew older. Most people pursue a state of perceived maturity like greyhounds chasing a stuffed rabbit around a dog track. But rock doesn't just encourage self-indulgence by design. Self-indulgence is actually part of its artistic process. Because it appeals to the young and this youthful audience requires an opportunity to share the artistic product through an exchange of self-indulgence, the result is a tendency for the art form itself to have an integral self-indulgent component. In short, self-indulgence isn't merely a weapon of rebellion but a necessary requirement all on its own.

When Alanis Morissette stalks on stage and self-indulgently shrieks her outrage over demanding parents — or more likely a demanding society — in *Perfect*, or over the lover who jilted her in *You Oughta Know*, there are thousands, even millions of fans, who feel delight in the rebellion inherent in this outrage and the release of their own repressed need for self-indulgence. If this all seems little more than gratifying a fatuous human need to be self-indulgent, consider the alternative. Imagine a world without self-indulgence. It's a world without rebellion, a world without an alternative to the status quo and, ultimately, a world without art.

Even in the artistic genre of rock music, there is a degree attached to self-indulgence. Self-confessional rock music is perhaps, by definition, the most self-indulgent of all. Morissette, in her work on JAGGED LITTLE PILL, is unabashedly succumbing to self-indulgence, especially in the sense that she wants to relate her apparent psychological enhancement in the wake of emotional tribulation. She wants her audience to know, through interviews and statements made after receiving awards, that she has created music in a state of spiritual awe and that she has found the fountain of creative integrity. All of these assertions are self-indulgent and oh so appropriate to the genre in which she has achieved popularity. Having maintained that all art requires self-indulgence and that rock requires even more self-indulgence to sustain its state of rebelliousness and its connection to a youthful audience, to say Morissette's work is self-indulgent is not the basis of any criticism. Rather, it perhaps explains why she has sold in excess of 15 million albums to an audience so able to identify with her life as portrayed in her words and music.

At the same time, this self-indulgence also provides an environment for some comparisons and contrasts between Morissette and rock 'n' rollers from the past who also utilized an unabashed self-indulgence to connect with the young then and in a continuing fashion of popularity today. To do so may explain, for instance, why Morissette has invited comparisons between herself and the late Jim Morrison of The Doors.

Strangely enough, Jim Morrison had already been dead for nearly three years by the time Alanis Morissette was born. But the level of candid self-confession and appropriate self-indulgence begs to be compared, just as their contrasts in style and private experience need to be mentioned. On the surface of it, there's a shaggy similarity between them, the brooding expression of poetic certainty, the dark hair which covers their faces on stage when they succumb to the emotion in their songs. To say Morissette resembles a sixties rocker on the surface, as opposed to the tattooed and pierced alternative version of the nineties, is to be obvious. Right down to the peace sign in her autograph, Morissette seems to be a blend of then and now somehow, as if rock, for all its travels hither and yon, just keeps coming back to the same self-indulgent location of rebellion and psychological tribulation.

For her part, Morissette admits that she grew up with the

likes of Joni Mitchell and Bob Dylan emanating from her parents' sound system. And although Morrison may not be mentioned specifically, there is a comparison to be made in the psychological edge to the music of The Doors and Morrison's ambition to be remembered, most of all, as a poet of his generation. Morissette, on the surface of it at least, seems to have similar aspirations and seems to feel justified within the context of grappling with her psychological demons. If Jim Morrison was struggling with Oedipal Complex, Morissette is wrestling with sexual repression. And if both — when inevitably critics gather to dismiss their work as post-adolescent self-indulgence, which they will without doubt — over-estimate the literary quality of their work, they will never be able to over-estimate the identification factor which their music and performances generate in their millions of fans.

"Sex, death, reptiles, charisma and a unique variant of the electric blues gave The Doors an aura of profundity that not only survived but has grown during the two decades plus since Jim Morrison's death," says *The New Rolling Stone Encyclopedia of Rock & Roll*. "By themselves, Morrison's lyrics read like adolescent posturings, but with his sexually charged delivery, Ray Manzarek's dry organ, and Robbie Krieger's jazzy guitar, they became eerie, powerful, almost shamanistic invocations that hinted at a familiarity with darker forces, and, in Morrison's case, an obsession with excess and death."

The history is well known even to a new generation of rock fans, due mainly to the popularity and success of the Oliver Stone film about the band which came out in 1991, the same year Alanis Morissette was grappling with the success and non-success of her first album, ALANIS. Briefly, The Doors formed in 1965 and by 1966 had recorded a demo tape and were working as the house band at the Whisky-A-Go-Go in Los Angeles. The gig at the club came to an abrupt end four months later, however, when they were fired for performing an explicit version of the *The End*, the most graphically Oedipal of Morrison's songs. In 1967, a single from their debut album, *Light My Fire*, reached number one, as did the album itself. While Morrison found himself on the cover of most music and teen magazines, FM stations began to play and analyze *The End*, trying to connect its apparent psychological meanings with the times and the prevailing counter culture.

The Doors were extremely successful. Their second album, STRANGE DAYS, went to number three, while their third, WAITING FOR THE SUN, wound up at number one. This album marked the introduction of the Lizard King, a persona Morrison adopted for himself which sent rock critics scurrying for some kind of accurate conclusion as to whether Morrison was parodying himself or utilizing the sensationalism which comes with exhibitionism cynically to sell records and maintain notoriety. Stories began to filter into the media about his various exploits. Not only was he arrested for public obscenity at a concert in New Haven in 1967, but also for disorderly conduct the next year over an incident on board an airplane which was headed for Phoenix. At the same time, music magazines even reported that he had purchased thousands of insects, beetles, at a pet store on Sunset Boulevard, with the intention of setting them free. When he did so, the bulk of them were killed in traffic. Whether this incident is true or not is not the issue. It reflects the self-indulgence and accompanying suspicion on the part of critics which would dog Morrison beyond the grave.

He was also arrested in Miami in 1969 for reportedly exhibiting "lewd and lascivious behavior by exposing his private parts and by simulating masturbation and oral copulation" during a concert. Strangely enough, the charges were eventually dropped when prosecutors failed to come up with any eye witnesses to the events. The result of the incident, however, was a reticence on the part of concert promoters to hire the band and a growing ambivalence on the part of Morrison himself about the lack of freedom in his celebrity status.

During this period, Morrison began to grow more and more involved with projects outside of the band, projects which demonstrated his ambition to be remembered as a poet. In 1970, a book of poetry, *An American Prayer,* was published privately, while in 1971 Simon and Shuster published *The Lords and the New Creatures*. The former enjoyed limited exposure until later that decade, seven years after Morrison's death, when the surviving members of The Doors set the poem to music. *Wilderness: The Lost Writings of Jim Morrison* was published in 1989. In addition to his poetry endeavors, Morrison collaborated on a screenplay with poet Michael McClure and directed a film, *A Feast of Friends*. Morrison had also produced films to coincide with the songs, *Break On Through* and *The Unknown Soldier*.

"Although Morrison expressed to friends and associates his wish to be remembered as a poet, overall his writings have found few fans among critics," the *Rolling Stone Encyclopedia* reports. "By then some felt, especially after *Touch Me*, that the band had sold out, and Morrison's dangerous persona was more often ridiculed than not. Critic Lester Bangs once tagged him 'Bozo Dionysus.'"

Emotionally and physically drained, it is reported, Morrison took an extended leave of absence from The Doors and went to Paris where he lived with his wife, Pamela, in seclusion, intending to write. It was there, when he was 27 years old, that Jim Morrison died of heart failure while in his bathtub. The fact his death was not made public until several days afterwards has only added to the legend of Morrison, and some fans do not believe he is truly dead. Pamela Morrison, reported to be one of the last people to see his body, died in Hollywood of a heroin overdose in 1974.

Despite being an obvious product of the late 1960s and early 1970s rock music world, The Doors have rarely been out of favor with rock fans. As each new decade reveals a different development in rock's ongoing evolution, The Doors continue to capture a place in the imagination of new groups of fans. In the 1980s, record sales of Doors music topped all previous sales figures, due in part to a popular biography of Morrison, *No One Here Gets Out Alive*, by Danny Sugerman and Jerry Hopkins, which appeared in 1980. This, coupled with new wave band treatment of Doors material and video airplay of Doors videos, contributed to their second wave of success. In the 1990s, happenstance and a continued production of Morrison material have continued this trend. For example, the 1995 reissue of *An American Prayer*, which includes a new track entitled *The Ghost Song* on which The Doors provided a musical backup to an old recording of Morrison reading from his work, has stimulated new interest. So too the Oliver Stone movie and the 1990 theft of Morrison's headstone in Paris, not to mention the group's induction into the Rock and Roll Hall of Fame in 1993.

As can be quickly seen, Jim Morrison might arguably be dubbed the king of self-indulgence. All the components are there to bestow on him such a title, from his frank sexuality and psychological admission of Freudian demons to his perpetual naivete that this kind of blunt sharing with the audience reflects an integrity of artistic motivation. The fact that it can be alleged by critics to be fabricated, contrived, or star-shaped only enhances the comparison with Alanis Morissette. In the way that *Time Magazine* referred to her lyrics as "rarely as smart as they seem to think they are," post-Morrison era analysts have condemned his work as mired in adolescent fantasy.

Yet Morissette and Morrison share a kind of integrity after all. Bearing in mind that rock music represents rebellion, a persistent challenging of the mores of conventional society, and bearing in mind that self-indulgence is, to some degree, at the root of all creative art, there can be little doubt that there always exists a perceived honesty in showing yourself in a self-confessional way to the audience which, in turn, is there to identify itself with what you are saying. This is the persistent cycle of self-indulgence, especially as it applies to the most self-indulgent medium of all, rock 'n' roll music. If some of us are embarrassed by this vicarious exchange of psychological candor between people like Morissette and her audience, as perhaps we were embarrassed when it was Jim Morrison and *his* audience, then perhaps that embarrassment derives from our absorption of the puritanical precept that self-indulgence has no place in an orderly society. And although this might be a sophisticated perch from which to view the human experience and the artistry which is part of that experience, we take that conventional view at our peril. To do so could mean that we have lost touch with the very basic truth that an audience appreciates its art *because* it is self-indulgent, not *despite* the fact.

What makes Morissette more refreshing when one considers this topic of self-indulgence is that she comes right out and admits it, at least the possibility that this is how her work can be received. She is rarely hesitant to admit that she is, as *Mojo Magazine* puts it, "a self-confessed psychobabble specialist," and, by extension, confesses broadly to the crime of self-indulgence which her genre sometimes proudly demonstrates.

"They tried to control me and I gave in to a certain extent," she said about her earlier Canadian dance period with MCA. "But back when I was 16 I wasn't ready to write songs this vulnerable. To write like this I think you have to be able to emotionally back it up. . . . Be vulnerable unapologetically. Though I did sometimes think, 'This is so self-indulgent, only 21-year-old former singer-dancer child actors are going to relate to it.'"

Even *Mojo* at least scratched the surface of relating this kind of self-indulgence to that offered by musicians from three decades earlier when it referred to the then upcoming and now well-known performance in Hyde Park on June 29, 1996 when Morissette performed with Eric Clapton, Pete Townshend, and Bob Dylan.

"Not inconspicuously, she'll be the only star-turn under 50," said *Mojo*. "Still, they'll all be pleased to hear they have the youngster's seal of approval; while conceding that she's not much good on legends of the '60s, she says she 'does her homework' on anyone she might share a bill with to check out not so much their musical compatibility as 'their aura, how they hold themselves.' These investigations have resulted in the down-turned thumb for a few big names already, so Eric, Pete and Bob can count themselves lucky. In fact, no study was required on the Dylan front. He was a part of Morissette's life from the cradle upwards. Her parents played him constantly throughout her childhood in Ottawa, Ontario. Then, in recent years, as she developed her writing towards its present level of confessional literacy, friends urged her to look again at artists like Dylan and Joni Mitchell 'who write from a really subconscious place' and she came to relish his enigmatic genius.

"However, Dylan could hardly be described as an influence on anything other than her cavalier approach to the orthodoxies of rhyme and scansion. Where he is often obscure, surreal and scorns ever to explain, she writes songs of startling autobiographical candor and is then willing to elucidate anything you may have missed, complete with a detailed exegesis of subtextual motivations," says *Mojo*.

But when the magazine suggests that Morissette may be rock's first practitioner of 'stadium therapy' to the masses," it can only be because they have not seen clearly the pale ghost of Jim Morrison lurking in the background, wrestling with *his* psychological demons before a throng of literally thousands.

And if one is looking for brutal honesty in that component of self-indulgence in Morissette's work, it's there in abundance. When *Spin* did its story on the new Canadian sensation, it told its readers about the "super-secret track at the very end of JAGGED LITTLE PILL. Search past track 13, the uncredited remix of *You Oughta Know*, until you get to 5:12, and you'll hear an a cappella Morissette seeking absolution from a lover whose house she has broken into — she takes a bath, plays his Joni Mitchell albums, puts on his cologne — as she sings, 'I shouldn't be here without permission / You might be home soon / Would you forgive me, love / If I laid in your bed?'" The track is saturated with reverb and possesses a chantlike, religious quality.

"That is the only song on the record that's not one hundred percent true," says Morissette. "I was staying in this guy's house in Hollywood and he wasn't there for a week. I remember being overly curious and sleeping in his bed. It felt eerie and unnerving; I also had kind of a crush on him. I get burned at the end of the song because if I had really snooped around as much as I wanted to, it would have been wrong. I probably would have found something I didn't want to find. I deserved it. So do you."

And that is another aspect of self-indulgence. Morissette knows as well as any of us that sometimes you have to be careful because you might find what you're looking for. Self-indulgence can disrobe an artist at times much more than the artist actually wants.

It's difficult to say whether songwriters such as Morissette, who are so close to the self-indulgence necessary for what they create, move beyond their sense that self-indulgence is what it is, but Morissette in particular counts on the honesty of psychological self-examination to form the foundation of her rapport with her audience. As Peter Howell noted in the *Calgary Herald*, "Besides deliverance, another of the things that Morissette really wants is 'intellectual intercourse,' a phrase from her opening song that's emblazoned on her official T-shirts being sold in the lobby."

Minneapolis-St. Paul Star Tribune writer Jon Beam's interview with Morissette reveals that at least Morissette is aware that her audience relates to "the release" she has written into the autobiographically psychological cream of the songs on JAGGED LITTLE PILL. Asked if the song *You Oughta Know* was written about revenge or release, she replied, "Release. If it was written for revenge, I think I'd be telling everyone his name. I would never mention his name. That goes for any song on the record. There are a lot of people I write about, but I would never mention any names. I haven't talked to him. I have reason to believe that he doesn't know it's about him. (Now) I'm secretly grateful to him for walking away from a relationship that wasn't very healthy."

Nor is Morissette comfortable with the notion that the candor she shares with audiences is rage. She dislikes that characterization. "I think it's predictable and one-dimensional. In time, people will realize it's not accurate. Truly, if some were to listen to the whole album, they'd know it's not about an angry person." She'll concede this much only: "I have an anger within me. It's one facet of my person." Instead of a preponderance of anger, she prefers to assume that her music reaches out and finds a place of identification in her audience. "Because people are relating to me. I don't think I'm the kind of artist who comes across as 'I'm a star, you can idolize me.' I come across as 'I'm human, you can relate to me.' I'm saying what a lot of people would want to say but would be far too embarrassed to say it. I had been too embarrassed to say it. I wrote it from a very dysfunctional part of my subconscious that I rarely indulge . . . ."

It's ironic that the contrasts Morissette has with the late Jim Morrison connect so well to the comparisons. By contrasts, one has to include the obvious gender difference, contradictions in career happenstance — Morissette's third album climbed to number one, while Morrison and the doors achieved that pinnacle on their first album — and Morrison's succumbing to drugs of various kinds, a world Morissette seems disinclined to favor. But regardless of those various contrasts, one cannot regard Morissette closely at times without noticing Morrison's ghost hovering in the background somehow, a comparison of emotionally charged stage presence perhaps, even those leather pants and the shaggy dark hair. But it's much more than that. It's the psychological confession in the musical presentation and the self-indulgence of that confession, a self-indulgence to which audiences have traditionally responded for years now, embracing it as something with which they can closely identify. Rock music is self-indulgence. Rock music and self-indulgence is rebellion. It's all part of the artistic canvas generations of young people have wanted to scrutinize since the dawn of rock 'n' roll. So they can move inside the canvas themselves, if only for a brief, vicarious hour or two.

An integral part of the subject matter in the songs on JAGGED LITTLE PILL is what Morissette learned from life in the chronological period between her two Canadian album recordings and the timespan after the second album failed to meet expectations. The period in question came on the heels of the success of her album ALANIS, then continued through the months spent recording the second album in Canada, NOW IS THE TIME. It was a period of flux for Morissette, some ups, some downs, hard work and confusion about her future, problems with relationships, a change of setting from Ottawa to Toronto, a period of persistent questioning about what she should do now with a life which included its creative demons.

According to the *Ottawa Citizen*'s hometown profile of Morissette, the second album turned out to be "a real grind, eight months of almost daily sessions in Howe's basement." The *Ottawa Sun's* Paul Cantin also reports that Morissette was up against some harrowing demands in life, that she found it difficult returning to school life, perhaps that the stage was now set for the various dynamics in her life which would lead to the self-confessional material on JAGGED LITTLE PILL.

"It was tricky for her, to keep her grades and going to school," recalls Stephan Klovan. "When someone has just been to the Junos and just won most promising singer and three days later, they are sitting in a physics class — it is quite a transition. It was frustrating that she couldn't have the social life of the average kid at Glebe. But she was getting so much more that it was worth it. And she also knew the sacrifice would pay off later on."

By now many media sources have reported Morissette's period of dating Dave Coulier of television's *Full House* and *America's Funniest People.* As late as the end of 1996, *People Weekly* sought him out for a comment on the new superstar, to embellish their report about her as one of the 25 most intriguing people of 1996. *People,* acknowledging that Coulier had dated her for approximately a year "on and off," reported that Coulier assured them JAGGED LITTLE PILL's "bitterness" was not part of her personality. "She has a great sense of humor. She's very introspective, but at the same time a bright and happy person," he said.

Klovan suggests, however, that the match raised a few eyebrows. "She met him in Montreal at the hockey all-star game and he is a big fan. They clicked and hit it off. When I met Dave, I had to admit their personalities meshed quite well. It is always easy to judge people and say: 'He's twice her age,' but they really seemed to have a good relationship while it lasted, and had a lot of fun. That's what it is all about."

Meanwhile, the "grind" of the second album went on and many consider it the album which subtly shifted Alanis in the direction she would take more radically on JAGGED LITTLE PILL. "It was a turning point album," says collaborator Serge Cote. "Alanis was growing up . . . from a teeny-bopper to an adult. She wanted to change."

In Morissette's mind, the second album was supposed to be the one that increased the distance between her and the dance tunes. The lyrics became more aggressive and more personal. Cote and Klovan agree on her desire to change her direction. "We kind of went with the flow of things," said Klovan. "The direction Alanis wanted to go in. It wasn't that drastic a difference. It was definitely a less-dance album than the first one. That was sort of fine with me . . . Alanis didn't want to go too dancey. She didn't want to be the dance queen. She wanted to write more serious type songs."

Morissette ended up caught in the middle between image-making and the honesty she wanted to put into her own music.

"This time I wanted to prove I could actually write the songs. More than anything, I wanted to prove it to myself, just wanted to bare my soul in the songs," she told *Toronto Sun* writer Rick Overall in October of 1992, just after the album's release. But according to Louise Reny, the pressure to be something else was relentless. "She's got the record company and people telling her 'you've got to look better. We want you to look like a little pop queen.' They want everybody to have boob jobs and be skinny and beautiful . . . you have to be *sooo* self-confident to get over that."

Such self-confidence seems to be earned in the lyrics to *Real World.* Serge Cote reports that *MuchMusic* balked at the video for *Real World* — "That's not Alanis, that's not dance" — a song testifying to the discovery of her "own voice":

> Life is so intense now, not much common sense now...
> I can make decisions with no one else believin' me
> I just look inside me
> 'cause I've got my own voice to guide me
> It came in a dream, a light so extreme
> A voice in my head, and it says
> "Step Inside The Real World"
>
> — *Real World*

Life "is not a game," she sings in the chorus, "it's a revelation." There would be many more games and revelations before she would rehearse this theme of self discovery on JAGGED LITTLE PILL.

The second album was not a complete disaster, for it did sell 50,000 copies in Canada, which is gold status. And the single *Emotion Away* initially leaped onto the charts, helped out by a video shot in Rome. Still, in contrast to the first album, sales were considered only modest. Said Howe, "In hindsight, I think we were in the middle of the road. We fell halfway between pop and dance. We weren't dance enough to appeal to the club people. And it wasn't pop enough for pop people . . . It was just kind of stuck in between genres. I'm very proud of that album too. But for whatever reason, it is impossible to predict or guess why people didn't buy something. If I could have done things differently, I would have gone more in the dance direction for that album."

Klovan, however, holds a different view, has speculated that the album was too similar to its predecessor. "Maybe the music was too much of a rehash of what the first album was. It wasn't different enough that people sat up and noticed it. I think that was a bit discouraging for Alanis. She had tasted such great success, and it almost came too easily. When the second one didn't do quite as well, it was almost a little bit of a reality check. I think she had expected this huge success to continue. She always put up a bit of a brave front and when that album kind of fizzed out, she realized she had to make some changes."

Although Morissette had chalked up 200,000 in sales on the albums, she was not in a financially lucrative situation. For his part, Howe reported receiving payment for his work in the form of recording budgets. "Even though she sold over 200,000 records, we were so heavily in debt with the record company. So we never got any actual royalties. The only money we received was the money to record the albums with." Klovan too stated later that the enterprise was "successful for her creatively, not financially."

Among the changes Morissette contemplated by the end of 1992 was whether or not she should attend university, whether or not she should exchange music for a different future. A factor in her deliberations was her acceptance at the University of Ottawa, the University of Toronto, and Carleton University, also in Ottawa. In the end, however, with MCA's John Alexander still expressing faith in her, she opted to continue on with her music career.

It was Alexander who connected Morissette with her present manager Scott Welch, known for his career transformation of Paula Abdul from a cheerleader into a popular dance act. Alexander's mission in approaching Welch was to attempt to get Welch to come up with an American release for Morissette's two Canadian albums, ALANIS and NOW IS THE TIME. At first, though impressed with Morissette's voice, he put the two Canadian releases on hold. It was important to him that he meet Morissette as well. In the end, he decided it was best for Morissette to begin afresh by leaving the first two albums behind.

"He sent me the records and I thought they were really good pop records," said Welch in the *Ottawa Sun* feature on Alanis. "I thought she has an amazing voice. I listened to them, I put it aside. I told him I was going to New York and he said: 'I'll bring her down.' I had dinner with her, and I was just knocked out by her. First of all, she is just a great friend . . . Friendships are meeting people halfway, and that's how she is. It's never me, me, me. You don't get many people who are just good people. My partner has been around for a long time, he managed Prince through the PURPLE RAIN years. You know, his attitude is, we only want to work with good people. We have turned down a lot of really financially rewarding clients, but he and I both want to have a life. I do not want to be called at three in the morning to bail somebody out of jail, or have scream-out matches, you know. She's just a good person. I just knew I wanted to work with her. What happened from there, she delivered. I said I think if we really want to see if this woman can blossom into something spectacular and stand on her own two feet, I think we shouldn't worry about licensing these records (the two Canadian releases). I think we should let her see if she is going to become a songwriter."

Both Klovan and Howe were left behind, although in later interviews both maintain they wanted to resume their own careers anyway, and Morissette was moved to Toronto, where, with modest financial support from Alexander, she was to collaborate with new songwriting partners and, at the same time, gain some of the life experiences that might appropriately find room in her music.

Said Welch, "I was beginning to believe she had reached a point creatively where she needed to work with fresh people. I think Leslie's records are great pop records. It's just that everybody changes producers because you need a different dynamic, a different spark. She wasn't this 14 or 15-year-old pop girl. She was a young woman with her own sensibilities. "I said, let's move her out of the house, away from Ottawa, some new surroundings, and let's get some new life experiences. Because that's what people write from. So we moved her to Toronto and she got a really crummy apartment, just like most of us did when we were 18, and she got by on macaroni and cheese."

From her third-floor walk-up in the Beaches area of Toronto and while gazing in despair at nearby Lake Ontario, she found a strange form of inspiration for her music. Morissette has called the two years she lived in Toronto the lowest time of her life. It is here where Morissette admits she endured a number of unhappy relationships with men which would eventually find a point of release in some of the songs on JAGGED LITTLE PILL. The provocation for *You Learn* perhaps occurred during this period:

> I recommend getting your heart trampled on to anyone
> I recommend walking around naked in your living
> room
> Swallow it down (what a jagged little pill)
> It feels so good (swimming in your stomach)
> Wait until the dust settles
>
> — *You Learn*

Speculation in the media has been even more intense as to the identity of the older man in *You Oughta Know*, whether he too was a factor in her life when she lived in Toronto or whether it was a relationship from her Ottawa days. Towards the end of 1996, when Morissette grew publicity shy and turned down most interviews, media sources hungry for another story launched their searches for the identity of the jilting lover, the "Mr. Duplicity" named in the song:

> You seem very well, things look peaceful
> I'm not quite as well, I thought you should know
> Did you forget about me Mr. Duplicity
> I hate to bug you in the middle of dinner
> It was a slap in the face how quickly I was replaced
> Are you thinking of me when you fuck her
>
> —*You Oughta Know*

But Morissette wasn't about to blow the whistle. Even during the period when she was regularly interviewed and asked about the lover in question, she was vehement that she would not give his name, especially since the songs were about release rather than revenge. "That's what people are misconstruing," she told Julene Snyder of *Bam*. "Because of the anger and how cutting some of the lyrics are, they presume that I Federal Express these songs to the people they're about and force them to listen to it. But I don't do that. A few people that the songs are inspired by — for them to even think for a minute that it's about them — well, that in and of itself says something about that person." She did admit to *Spin* in November 1995, however, that she had never been in a positive relationship and cited examples of "dalliances with older men who were 'emotionally unavailable' to her."

The months she spent in Toronto seem to have been frustrating for Morissette romantically. Another form of frustration arose from a failure in the collaborative songwriting process. David Baxter, creative director of Peer Publishing, a music company there where Morissette collaborated with various songwriters through his "Music Works" program, told the *Ottawa Citizen*, however, that "For as long as I knew her, she was always hard-working and upbeat . . . she was just determined to improve as a songwriter and worked all the time." He reported as well that a song she wrote with Steve Haflidson "made the hair stand up on peoples' necks." The song in question, *Gone*, was slated to come out in 1996 on an album Haflidson was scheduled to release. Baxter admits, though, that she was not satisfied with how it was going in Toronto, despite the fact Morissette credits his program with improvements in her writing. "She felt she needed a complete break, she thought about New York but decided to move to L.A. She never would have made it in Toronto, it's too nice a place."

Morissette admits she was discouraged. "I would write in the way I wrote JAGGED LITTLE PILL, and I have vivid memories of writing and then just looking up at the person I was writing with and they would be shaking their head, saying: 'You can't do that.' And I would say: 'I have to go!' And I wouldn't finish the song, or I would finish it and nothing would be personal, and in my own mind I would disown it. There are so many disowned songs of mine out there, that I have absolutely no connection with. I worked almost seven days a week, writing with everybody, trying to get into the whole songwriting part of it. I would write alone, write with people, write with three people and demo, and I just tried everything. There was really no one I was connecting with in a cerebral, creative way at all. It became very disheartening. The whole collaborative process, I almost threw it out the window."

Paul Cantin, in relating these frustrations in the *Ottawa Sun*, maintains that her would-be collaborators had different agendas. "She was in search of an artistic identity, and the hired-gun writers were in search of a lucrative hit." This was Welch's view. "When you write with a lot of writers, that's how they earn their money, so they are like: We gotta get something on the record! She was like: 'I don't know what I'm gonna do yet. I'm just writing.' It was like she was in it for the spirit of the writing and other people were in it for: 'Let's write something we can put on your next record. Her frustration was she had a lot more to say, but because she was still growing, she wasn't really a great musician yet, she was frustrated she had a whole bunch of ideas but couldn't translate them yet."

At the same time, Morissette continued with television, debuting as the hostess of a CBC-TV program called *Music Works* in 1994. Although she did not return the next year (Pat Mastroianni became the host in 1995), Morissette is credited with both the show's title and its mission statement. "You can have a lot of talent in the music business, but if you want to succeed it takes that, plus an enormous amount of work — from that ideology the show was called *Music Works*," said producer Adele Cardamone. Each episode of the program featured a Canadian band or artist performing in an Ottawa warehouse studio space before a live audience. Although designed to be slick and polished, it was also set up to have a "raw feel," something that reflects a musician's point of view. The program featured each artist performing five songs in their own half-hour spotlight.

Although there is little doubt Morissette gained valuable experience with her tenure in Toronto, and as the result of a similar trip to Nashville for collaboration, the experiences were ultimately not helpful. Undeterred, Morissette began commuting to

Los Angeles for stints with writers there, termed sometimes as writing blind dates, the objective of which was to finally match her up with the right person.

Los Angeles provided some bad and some good. But Los Angeles became part of Morissette's creative destiny. Los Angeles was where JAGGED LITTLE PILL was born.

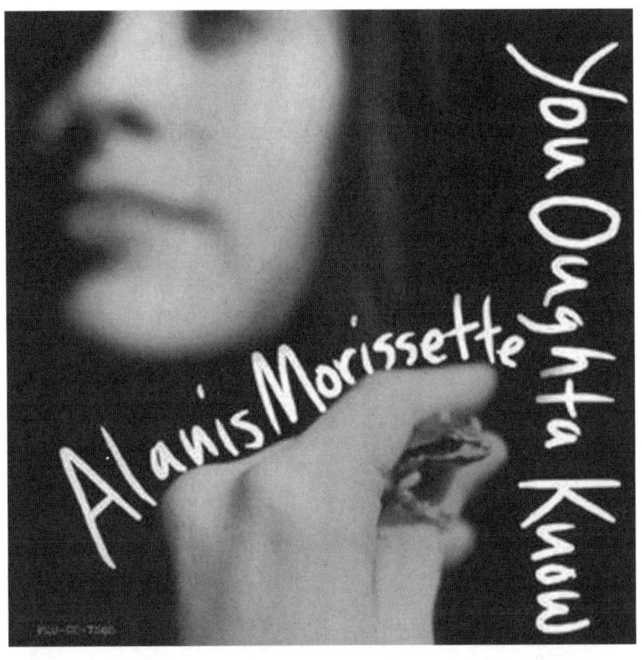

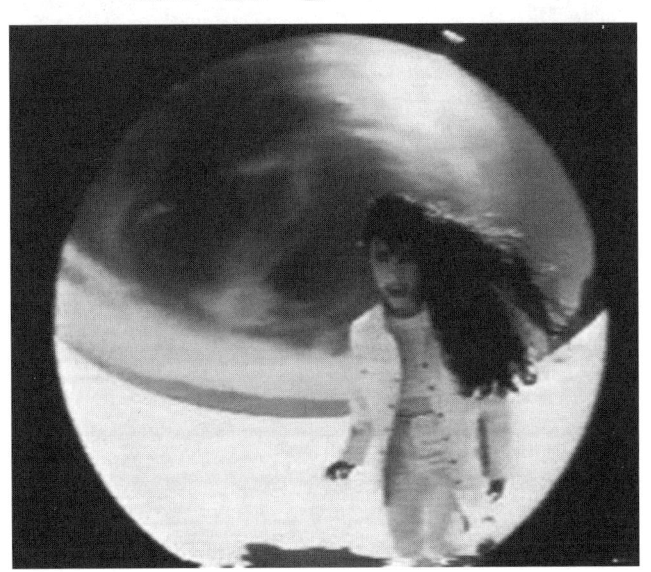

"Alanisphere" from the video for You Oughta Know.

·five·

Not The Doctor

I've had all sorts of love, I've had evacuation love, dependency love and I used to be a control freak.

— *Alanis Morissette*

Hey what are you hungry for
I don't want to be the glue that holds your pieces
together
I don't want to be your idol
See this pedestal is high and I'm afraid of heights
I don't want to be lived through
A vicarious occasion
Please open the window

— *Not the Doctor*

One of the factors which makes Alanis Morissette the perfect rock poet for an era which may become known as the age of irony is that she is a self-confessed student and practitioner of what is termed "psychobabble." *Mojo Magazine* even went so far as to suggest that "Morissette may be rock's first practitioner of 'stadium therapy.'" She and her audiences, within the context of the modern tendency towards self-analysis and "getting control of one's life," are made for each other. Morissette takes to the stage with the intention of releasing her neuroses, and the audience, in accepting this release, has a tendency to shrug off, at least temporarily, their own neuroses as well.

Part of Morissette's amazing success since the release of JAGGED LITTLE PILL may be the apt timing of this psychological marriage between a performer with her kind of frankness and an audience which speaks her particular language. Her audience has arguably been ready for this kind of free emotional exchange for some time now. In terms of the cynicism which emerges in a generation with little to believe in, there is one potential solace for the millions of young people on the verge of drowning in all the irony which seems to result: when there isn't much out there to believe in, well, the least you can do is believe in yourself.

In interview after interview, profile after profile, regardless of its time-frame, whether it speaks of what she was like in the earlier stages of her career or whether it concentrates on who she is now in the wake of JAGGED LITTLE PILL, Morissette is described variously as a "self-possessed" person, confident, a person who knows who she is and who elevates the concepts of honesty and self-knowledge above most other human qualities. Consequently she appears surprisingly mature in most ways. Even as a child, she seems sure of where she is going and what she wants to do, demonstrates few qualms about taking steps to achieve her goals and handles herself well in demanding situations. And, these days, on stage, she conveys these characteristics to her audience. She seems to be saying: "See? I've got *my* shit together. I'll bet you can too." Her audience, for its part, wants to believe this is true. Because, beyond this particular achievement, there isn't much else in their lives that is as certain or assured. Control over ourselves is perhaps the only realistic goal to which we can all aspire now that the world of information highways and free market as religion has removed so much else from our control.

Morissette, at times, sounds like a psychology textbook herself. According to *Mojo*, she commonly uses expressions like "I take responsibility for that" or "I have to be patient with that." Even when pressed to elucidate about her affairs of the heart, she has responded with "I've had all sorts of love, I've had evacuation love, dependency love and I used to be a control freak." In the same article, asked if she has held back details of some personal crises in her music, she admits this is so. "Yes," she says. "A few. People think these songs are so confessional, what could she possibly have left? But I still have boundaries. There's a huge element of self protection there, more now than ever, I think."

Ironically, though, that's part of the appeal to her audience. She may be exercising a powerful forthrightness in her self-confessional delivery on the one hand, but on the other she's demonstrating control over self which is just as appealing as the candor.

New York Times' music critic Jon Pareles also reports the psychological aspect of her music, and the way she turns to psychological terminology to define it. "Forthrightness, linked to catchy tunes, has made Ms. Morissette hugely successful. The songs on JAGGED LITTLE PILL vent her rage and insecurity . . . Morissette, for her part, responds that "I've just found myself with a certain sense of fearlessness about my vulnerability. I found that the more truthful and vulnerable I was, the more empowering it was for me."

Her interview in *Spin* develops the same message, showing that Morissette is saying things in her lyrics that are often relegated to the subtext of pop music. Outlining the frustration that women performers have in being deemed angry as a movement by the media, when they are seeking instead only a long overdue freedom in honesty, Morissette stands out because of the casual way in which she "carves out space for a broad emotional range (which) is typical of men: She simply assumes it."

"Being able to express both your masculine and feminine sides is a great advantage," says Morissette. *Spin* took note of additional indications of her unusual poise for her age. "Because of her ample confidence, not to mention the cross-legged Buddha posture she's assumed, it's easy to forget that Morissette has only walked the earth for 21 years." From *Spin*'s perspective, part of the allure of this maturity is Morissette's willingness to admit that, creatively especially, she's been on the very bottom of things and views that area of residence as the starting point of something better. It's almost an annoying indication of psychological health, especially from the standpoint that many of us do not reach this conclusion until much later in life. "You have to reach a point that you're so consumed by whatever it is that you can't take it anymore, and until you reach that point you just coast along like a bottom-dweller," she has said.

No wonder the audiences are drawn to her. She's not only saying she's been through the same tribulations as everyone else out there, but that she's turned them to advantage by transforming them into a growth experience. "The reaction of the audience has been so amazing and open," she told *Rolling Stone* writer David Wild. "It's comforting and bittersweet to know that I'm not the only one who's gone through these things. At the same time it's a little disturbing that apparently there's a lot of people out there having gone through such painful things. The reaction has been pretty intense." The intensity of what passes between Morissette and her audience may be the faith that there is a light at the end of the tunnel, where pain and hard times possess at least a potential for alleviation. "A lot of times when you're immersed in something painful," says Morissette, "you don't realize there's any lesson. A lot of what I wrote about was difficult times from which I walked away a better person."

Adds Wild, "Morissette connects with her audience in a way that — when viewed without fashionable cynicism — is moving. The dynamic is less like a concert than modern-rock group therapy with Morissette serving as a sort of twentysomething Joni Mitchell backed by thrashy guitar. Despite having a song called *Ironic,* she's as unironic an artist as they currently come. 'Thank you for understanding,' she meaningfully tells the crowd before launching into her encore number, *Perfect,* an anthem about the pressure of youth."

Even Madonna, the superstar CEO of Morissette's Maverick

Records label, claims she was drawn to Morissette's music by "her honesty, her pain, her hopefulness." Adds Madonna, "She reminds me of me when I started out: slightly awkward but extremely self-possessed and straightforward. There's a sense of excitement and giddiness in the air around her — like everything's possible, and the sky's the limit."

Glen Ballard has a similar idea of the young Morissette, especially where it focuses on their songwriting collaboration. "What struck me about Alanis was that she was so incredibly self-possessed. I just connected with her as a person, and, almost parenthetically, it was like 'Wow, you're 19?' She was so intelligent and ready to take a chance on doing something that might have no commercial application. Although there was some question about what she wanted to do musically, she knew what she didn't want to do, which was anything that wasn't authentic and from the heart."

Whether Maverick or Reprise somehow was able to anticipate the wonderful marketing opportunity which existed in the potential for Morissette's psychological audience to respond to an equally psychological Morissette or whether they just were infected by Morissette's need for emotional honesty is difficult to say. Nonetheless, the same approach to Morissette, the same acknowledgment of the self-possession, is contained in biographical material they prepared for the media about their new musical discovery.

"To those who think the generation that came of age in the 1980s lacks focus, here's one bit of advice . . . take a pill — a JAGGED LITTLE PILL!" says a release from Maverick. "Although she only recently passed her 20th birthday, Alanis Morissette's Maverick debut proves she possesses a wealth of insight and an off-kilter sense of humor that's at once untainted and mature. 'People have always said I was an old soul,' says Alanis. 'They said I was always a little more intense and introspective than everyone was used to seeing girls be, so they didn't know where to categorize me.' It all boils down to this one fact: "I want to walk through life instead of being dragged through it.'

"That's a pretty accurate description of the jarringly honest, frequently provocative songs on JAGGED LITTLE PILL, Alanis'

Maverick debut. The native of Ottawa, Canada uses her own experiences — from a Catholic school upbringing, to her many travels through Europe as a youth, to her years as a teenager living alone in Toronto — as a springboard for some striking universal statements. In the incisive *All I Really Want* (on which her self-aware observations are set against a swirling psychedelic canvas), Alanis pleads for fulfillment of needs both physical and psychic, while the stirring *Not The Doctor* offers a steely-eyed declaration of emotional independence. 'Most of the songs are, in a roundabout way, actually addressed to myself; there's a certain aspect of the songs that's very confessional, very unadulterated,' she allows. 'I wrote some of the songs and woke up the next day not even remembering I'd done them — almost like a steam-of-consciousness. It was a very unfettered, spiritual experience."

Whether the Maverick approach to publicizing Morissette was nothing more than brilliant marketing or the coming together of various spiritual factors, even early media coverage of Morissette's rocketing good fortune with JAGGED LITTLE PILL has not missed the message of empowerment or the fact she has connected in an unusual way with her audience and the various tribulations the times and circumstances have bestowed on its members. A fine example is Jeff Spurrier's article in the October 1995 issue of *Details*.

"Alanis Morissette's *You Oughta Know* is every ex-lover's worst nightmare, the most unwelcome of three a.m. phone calls, it's full of blistering accusations and unanswerable questions, like its acid catchphrase-in-the-making, 'Are you thinking of me when you fuck her?' In the video, she wails, snarls, and sneers; trudges through a symbolic desert wasteland; and makes three changes of costume — just in case you miss the theme of shedding skin and violent personal renewal. By the time she lies down in a field of flowers at the end, you hope she's exorcised her personal demons. She sure has awakened yours. It's the empowerment clip of the day, a raspy anthem for all those inner children out there who refuse to get over it.

"Alanis didn't simply reinvent herself to make *You Oughta Know* and the album it came from, JAGGED LITTLE PILL. She cut down to the bone, stripped out her innards, and held them up for everyone to enjoy. Self-excavation the Henry Rollins way is a dangerous game, but at her best Alanis comes across like a more repressed Liz Phair, a less disturbed Sinead O'Connor, a Marianne Faithfull who never shot junk. At worst, she sounds like Edie Brickell on a bad day."

What adds to this apparent assessment is Morissette's ability to confess, not only in song, but in interviews. She'll admit about some psychological troubling recollections about stealing boyfriends, about breakdowns and therapy, about previous sexual exploitation of her in the music business and how easy it was to feel compelled to seek approval when she was young.

"Where Disco Alanis used to flaunt décolletage during her bubblegum days, now she won't wear clothes that highlight her butt at the expense of her songs," wrote Spurrier. "And anyway, she says, she'll never fit society and the media's standards of perfection, so why try?" He related how Morissette thought her youthful accomplishments were "like sugar to a diabetic."

"I'd say 'Thank you' for a compliment and think, 'You don't know how terrible I am!' It was a little bit of a drug for me. I wound up with all this adulation, and at that age you don't know what self-esteem is," said Morissette. And the psychological revelations go on, her habit of stealing boyfriends from friends her own age, purely for the conquest of it because, in truth, she found them too immature. "The only way I felt desirable was when a man would leave his girlfriend for me. I wish I could go back and apologize to all the girls I did that to. And if I ever dated guys my own age, it would only last about a week."

"When she was fourteen she was trying to be forty — signing contracts, making videos, revelling in adult approval," said Spurrier. "Now she's twenty-one and trying to be twelve, doing all the things her Catholic childhood and self-imposed perfection wouldn't allow. Everything, that is, apart from smoking tobacco, drinking, injecting, snorting, or doing caffeine. She even wears stick-on tattoos: 'Part of my fear of commitment.' It's a funny kind of abandon."

Morissette's life has had a number of psychological turning points. One of them, perhaps, took place when she was flying home from Los Angeles to Ottawa, in December of 1994, when, as Spurrier puts it, "the emotional costs she had avoided for so long came due."

"I was writing my fifty-sixth Christmas card on the plane," says Morissette, "when I had a head-on anxiety attack. I just bawled my eyes out and started shaking and wanted to faint. It scared the living shit out of me."

Says Spurrier, "Similar uncontrollable crying jags and fainting spells followed, and she checked herself into a hospital, admitting to herself that she was losing it. Hypnosis and therapy helped to release years of blocked emotions, feelings she didn't even have a name for. When she started working on PILL, the songs came spilling out like automatic writing, some of them so unbidden that she doesn't even remember putting the words on paper. Far from her own pop confections, these were discordant, off-kilter tunes about rejection, betrayal, guilt, and — yes — oral sex."

The recurring theme in Morissette's revelations about herself and the music which emerged when she finally grappled with her personal demons are fairly standard psychological fair, which only enhances the ease with which her audience can relate to them when she performs.

"When I was younger and doing what I did in Canada, it was driven by what other people thought," she told writer Lorraine Ali in Los Angeles. "It's really fascinating and enticing to be sixteen and do as much promo as you can, but as time when on, I realized it's not at all what people perceive it as. I'm glad that happened, because now, when there's a decision to be made on whether I should do something or not, I base it on whether I truly want to do it or not as opposed to how many people are gonna see it. I'm glad I went the other way for a few years." Do her lyrics scare people? "Yes. Particularly people who knew me when I was younger. When I was younger, I was a lot more worried about people's perception of me, I wanted their approval, so I always came across happy. So when they finally heard this more honest part of me, I think they were like, 'yikes!' I think for the most part though, most people are happy to hear that I'm being honest. . . . I never considered myself to be a very radical kind of person. That's why the response to my album is a little overwhelming. People are saying to me, 'you're saying things no one's ever said,' and I'm thinking, 'Am I really?' I'm not doing anything that isn't just human."

There's a side of Morissette that seems perpetually bemused by the response she has received to JAGGED LITTLE PILL. Maintaining that the music contained on the album reflects her psychological emergence from the dark days of seeking approval and all the repression which often occurs in that circumstance, she seems as puzzled by how the music happened as she does by her audience's appreciation of it.

"There are so many people coming up to me, saying, 'I thought I was abnormal, and after hearing what you say, I realize now that I'm human, that it's okay,'' she told J.D. Considine of the *Chicago Sun-Times*. "In retrospect, now — I was so immersed in the record when I wrote it that I couldn't see beyond my hand, holding it in front of me — but in retrospect, I see that record as a response. It's a response to what I was immersed in when I was younger; it was a response to society; it was a response to the way I was treated, the way I was brought up. The way I was taught to be."

Morissette brings this "response" to her audience, along with a healthy dose of psychological identification so that they can see the potential for their own release, their own response. "*You Oughta Know* was almost the first time that I allowed myself to write exactly how I felt," she told Karen Bliss in *Canadian Musician*, "because I'm sort of an analytical thinker and a lot of times, I don't want to disrespect somebody — that whole passive/aggressive thing — so with a lot of the songs, I finally had the opportunity not only to be honest with myself, but in some cases, with the people I was upset with or the situation. I feel the reason I'm still feeling okay now is because psychology saved me. If I couldn't figure out why I was confused or why I was sad or upset, I'd still feel that way, so I thought the only way I could transcend it was to understand it. And over the past few years, through writing songs, I've dealt with a lot of things that I hadn't really thought about or was afraid to think about."

While Morissette focuses on "transcending" her repression, on the fact that "psychology saved" her, she is well aware that the members of her various audiences are absorbing these developments and applying them to themselves. "It's almost like I felt that by my being that introspective, that other people would be compelled to be introspective about their own lives too, and apparently that's what's happening," she said during a radio interview in Hawaii in August 1995. "And that's beautiful for me, that's, you know, even outside of music there's nothing more exciting for me than seeing someone growing, or figuring things out, or communicating. And — and the fact that this record is prompting people to do that is just so satisfying for me."

Morissette speaks of a duality in her nature, the one more focused on approval, the other concerned with emotional honesty and release. "I think the most difficult part for me was thinking that some of the lyrics that were so honest that a few people hearing it might actually get hurt by it. But, you know, I had to think about that and say that this was something that I really had to release, for my peace of mind. And a lot of the reasons why this anger, or this confusion, or any of the emotions, for that matter, is so overt is because a lot of it was repressed for so long. And if finally I had this opportunity to release all of it and I again denied myself of that and only allowed sixty percent of it to come out, then again I'd just sort of be perpetuating my — you know, just holding everything back again, and at some point I was going to explode . . . or implode."

A schizophrenic experience? "Yeah, I sort of had two different sort of — where the dualities in me started to arise, I think, when I was younger, was that I spent a lot of time with people my age just for that youthful, exuberant kind of spirit, you know? And then I spent an equally large amount of time with adults, and — and talking to them on a real intellectual, cerebral sort of level. And, unfortunately, I think that the part that was the most difficult for me was just the fact that there was — there was no one person that I could get everything from — as far as a friend, or a boyfriend, or, you know, even a family member, and it was like — and I think there was such, there was such a separation between two parts of me and I was just — even a little bit today, I'm just — I'm just really waiting for the time when they can merge and live happily together. You know?"

At the root of Morissette's success with JAGGED LITTLE PILL may be popular acknowledgment of a duality in most modern young people which has traditionally been termed existential crisis. Her audience may view the album, with its candor, self-confession, emotional outrage and alleviation of repression, as the potential for their own triumph over that side of their nature which tows the line incessantly and kowtows to various societal forces which manipulate their lives on a daily basis. It may even reflect an alternative to an entire jaded age group which views irony as such a steadfast vacuum of basic belief that there seems to be no antidote to irony itself. In other words, if you finally deal with your own existential crisis, finally acknowledge what philosopher Jean-Paul Sartre described as the *en soi* and *pour soi* forces in your life, you can begin to address a solution to having so little control over that life and the alternative of self realization may then present itself, not to mention insisting upon a change in the world's direction towards disenfranchisement of its people as individuals.

Strangely enough, the cultural genre of rock music has always had that potential. It has always provided a showcase for that duality in all of us, on the one hand offering the rebellious side of our nature some solace, while, on the other, leaving us free to resume the normalcy of our day-to-day affairs. Rock music has always been able to permit us to dabble in our existential crises, often quite happily, while only infrequently inspiring us to seek real change.

Morissette's revelations in her interviews, in her recorded music on JAGGED LITTLE PILL, in her concert performances, all reflect classic existential crisis and the classic battleground between ego and super-ego which all of us endure, to varying degrees, in our lives. We are faced, from the cradle, with a choice between doing what the world wants us to do — *en soi* — and being motivated to do what we would actually personally and creatively prefer — *pour soi*. Often, the first force is the impact of our parents on our lives, in Freudian terms, the super-ego. We are trained to assimilate their values, mores, and opinions and these form the basic framework of our search for approval. In a sense, all approval we seek later in our lives is actually our parents' approval. What causes conflict in each of us, however, in often drastically varying degrees of intensity, is the impact of our own egos on what we have assimilated from our families. Sometimes, we rebel against those aforementioned values, mores, and opinions. As Morissette has outlined in her candid remarks about her own search for approval and her own psychological cure, we become aware of an apparent duality in our nature. One side of us wants to make our parents — by extension, our world — happy with us. The other wants to embark on a more honest voyage of self-discovery, self-fulfillment, and self-actualization.

Within the context of Morissette's impact on an entire generation of young people, there seems to be a sharing, between performer and audience, of a tremendous acknowledgment of a massive existential crisis of sorts. This may be remarkable enough on the psychological level, but it becomes even more staggering when one applies the theorem to the potential for cultural impact and even the possibility of political or societal change. It then represents a first step towards acknowledging that the social status quo which so capably manipulates us at this stage of our human history may be fraught with a self-interest which denies us our personal creativity and individualism. Once we understand the injustice in that state of affairs, we have embarked on a kind of concerted rebellion, a rekindling of our sense of ourselves as citizens in a world which is not only ours to grow in, but to which we have a wonderful responsibility. Suddenly, the generation immersed so completely in an age in which everything is ironic, in which there is little concept of social alternative, has a very real alternative for both social and personal change. Suddenly, there is reason to consider that there might be a movement underway. Suddenly, all that has been unsuitable as a basis for any kind of belief, has at least a glimmer of potential faith.

On the surface of it, this would seem to elevate Morissette to the level of messiah. This is not the intention. Instead, it points out that whatever concoction of societal pressures have come together to create it, Morissette's perceived honesty, admission of personal crisis, and frank outrage have somehow touched a nerve with a large audience which appears to have felt similar individual needs. Rather than leading this revolution of psychological candor, she is simply drawing our attention to it. It may be a final stroke of irony, that the most outspoken proponent of unironic irony has at least a passing function to bring the age of irony to the only kind of conclusion available to it, a cessation of the impotence implicit in its irony.

Nor is this a tangential theory. From the moment that JAGGED LITTLE PILL was born, the main thrust of the music's creation, its impact on millions of fans, and the history of how its performer came to be the person she is now have focused entirely on the release from confinement of her individual nature over the forces of the status quo, that is the pressure of the image-makers, the cynicism of the naysayers, and even the coincidental repression of her parents and their society. More importantly, the rather phenomenal appreciation an entire generation has lauded on this circumstance only reflects that they share the same sense of individual confinement and need for release from that confinement.

"Stadium therapy" it may be but it is now apparent that it has been a therapy an entire generation has needed. And depending on where music, honesty, mass psychology, and politics evolve from here, a generation, which has denied previously the possibility of any alternative, is now showing, in its own gentle outrage, at least a tentative indication that some kind of alternative might be possible after all.

Even by the time Alanis Morissette had decided she should move to Los Angeles, the various demons which repressed her remained locked inside her. The creative frustration and personal "duality" she struggled with in Toronto did not resolve themselves during her initial period in California. To make matters worse, happenstance made the transition from living in Canada to living in the United States a bit of an ordeal at first and, at the same time, served to elaborate somewhat on the basic cultural differences between the two countries.

The incident in question was a mugging at gunpoint. Morissette, who was living in the Santa Monica apartment of a friend, was accosted and forced to lie face down in the laneway.

Strangely enough, although the incident took place prior to her final decision to move there and although she confided to friends that she was "devastated" by the experience, it wasn't long afterwards that she recounted the event as almost a necessary learning experience, an important creative development, and, accordingly, she soon decided to move to Los Angeles permanently.

In so doing, she and her management associates seemed to indicate, not only that a gunpoint mugging is not all that untoward for a victim but that it is part of a growing up experience, which, if such a conclusion is to be believed, only demonstrates the kind of sheltered Canadian experience that Morissette was apparently willing to give up to gain its American alternative. Morissette would later blame her own Canadian personality — "my quiet confidence was misconstrued for this passivity" — for the mugging incident. And Scott Welch, her new manager, told Paul Cantin of the *Ottawa Sun* that the mugging was just part of the growing up experience too. "All this time, she is going through separating from her parents and growing up. She got robbed down here (in L.A.), she got robbed at gunpoint, and all those things normal kids growing up go through. I think the thing that sustained her was she knew John (Alexander) and I were really supportive. I mean, living away from home like that is like going to college. You're at college, man, it is scary for you, especially if you move to a new city and you don't know anybody," he said.

At any rate, if Morissette detected a distinct contrast in the culture between the United States and Canada, not even the mugging incident was going to deter her. She was still intent upon her quest to find a suitable songwriting partner who would unleash her creative potential. Although she had not found the songwriting assurance she was looking for, those connected with her during this period felt she was making progress, that she was showing evidence of growth.

"She'd go off to write with someone and everyone would call me after, saying: Man, there's something really special here," said Welch. "I hadn't seen her for a while and we went for lunch and she said: 'I've got a tape, I've got fifteen things I want to play for you.' And ten of them, you could start to see . . . turn into

JAGGED LITTLE PILL. You could see glimpses of things. I said: 'Man, you are on the right track. Just stay with it.''' Morissette, for her part, recalls that period as one of faith, even though she had little indication that the faith wasn't groundless.

Then, after a number of disappointments, Morissette was set up with veteran L.A. musician and producer Glen Ballard, what Abraham and Provencher in the *Ottawa Citizen* called "the musical equivalent of love at first sight." Said Morissette, "It came together in a terrific rush. Most of the time, I went in with some ideas, but the actual *song* would get written and recorded in one take. I'd sometimes go back to the studio the next day and not remember having done the song."

Ballard was no stranger to music. Born in Mississippi, he was originally a keyboardist. From a production standpoint, he had worked as a staff producer for Quincy Jones and worked with such "names" as Aretha Franklin, Natalie Cole, George Benson, Chaka Khan, The Pointer Sisters, Paula Abdul, Teddy Pendergrass, Curtis Stigers, Al Jarreau, James Ingram, and even Barbra Streisand. As well, he had worked with Earth, Wind & Fire, Philip Bailey, Patti Austin, K.T. Oslin, Jack Wagner, Wilson Phillips, and George Strait, not to mention Steven Tyler and Joe Perry of Aerosmith. Ballard is also known for his writing and arrangement of Michael Jackson's *Man In The Mirror*. Ballard has reportedly written or produced albums which have sold almost 100 million copies.

In a *Boston Globe* feature, Steve Morse describes Ballard as "soft-spoken and long-haired. The 43-year-old Ballard blends hippie ideals with a '90s pragmatism. Most of all, he reflects his background in one of American music's crossroads. 'Music is music,' says this Natchez, Miss., native who used to hear Jerry Lee Lewis and other legends in local roadhouses. 'I'm a musician first. I've been trained classically, but I grew up in the South around real blues players and real New Orleans jazz. So I've been informed from a lot of different places. And of course when the Beatles came into prominence, I was grooving on that. But there was something about the local music — people like Irma Thomas and others coming out of New Orleans and Memphis — that was incredible. The spirit of that music is with me today.'"

Ballard is of the school that he should honor a songwriter's need for personal expression. "I just feel solidarity with people who are trying to express themselves," he said. "It's so hard to get it just the way you want it. If I do anything well, I think it's to help nuance that. And with Alanis, she was so open to my contribution as a musician and I was able to stretch harmonically. I would play a weird chord, a ninth or an eleventh or a major seventh, and she never flinched. Because she's so musical, she embraced the new harmonic landscapes. We sort of enabled each other to be the best we could be. And we had a lot of fun. We laughed all the time. It was so intense, what was going on here, that the humor was intense too. It would be three o'clock in the morning and we had given all our blood, but we would be happily tired."

Both Ballard and Morissette have described the chemistry of their collaborative writing as nearly spiritual from the time in February of 1994 when they first met, a meeting set up by MCA Music, their publishing company. "I'm totally spoiled for life, no question, no doubt," Ballard said afterwards. "She has spoiled me for life of everything creatively. It is such a connection. We can just close our eyes and do it." Morissette has expressed the same point of view. "Glen had a certain history, as I had, and when we met, we immediately connected," she told David Wild of *Rolling Stone*. "We just started with a clean slate. It was the most spiritual experience either of us ever had with music. The whole thing was very accelerated and stream of consciousness." And she told *Mojo*, "Musically and cerebrally Glen and I were so on the same wavelength it all came together. It was all very visceral — and fast. What makes this relationship so magic for me is that a lot of what I would be talking about or thinking about or intellectualizing about — over intellectualizing about — Glen would say, 'Well, yeah?' to when most people would be, 'What are you talking about?' or 'God, would you stop analyzing!' We'd talk, and out of the conversation would come a song. We agreed that what was being said was more important than whether the words fit, technically speaking. There are a lot of instances where they don't fit. I don't care." Morissette even went so far as to suggest, because there was never anyone else in the studio when she and Ballard were writing, that she would not have been able to write so freely had there been more than just the two of them present.

She also suggested that the breakthrough song for them during this period was *Perfect*. "Glen and I were working on something else, which didn't make it onto the record. In the middle of it we turned to each other [she cartoons, eyebrows-raised, open-mouthed astonishment] and went off on this other song which would end up being *Perfect*. The words and music were written in about twenty minutes and we recorded it, the original demo that's on the album, that same evening. It was overwhelming. I think we finished it around one in the morning and we couldn't leave the studio 'til about five because . . . it was pretty scary. I was scared. . . . I'm such an analytical person and I didn't have any answer for it."

Ballard has made much of his first impressions of Morissette as an articulate and intelligent person, part of the reason they were able to get started writing within minutes of meeting. "I think there was an instant rapport, immediately," Ballard told Paul Cantin in the *Ottawa Sun*. "It wasn't awkward for any length of time. It was relaxed. It really is hard to tell you why. All I can tell you is it was one of those instant connections, and we didn't have the slightest problem getting work. That never happens. But in this case, that is exactly what happened."

Although much of their initial efforts did not make it onto an album, some of them songs which Morissette claims to favor, Ballard and Morissette knew very quickly that they were going to succeed as collaborators. Since that time, as songwriting partners, both of them have maintained that they both had something to prove to themselves and in the world of music generally. With shared but separate histories of pop music behind them, they were both ready for the franker honesty of the music contained on JAGGED LITTLE PILL. Both wanted to do something completely different from what they had achieved in the past.

"They put us together, thinking that we'd probably come up with some more pop dance stuff," Morissette has said. "When Glen and I got together, we knew immediately that this was something that was very special. We both started with a clean slate. It was like a sanctuary for us. We were finally in this environment where we could do whatever the hell we wanted to do, because there was no expectation. He had a lot of success in the past, and me being in America, no one had heard of (my) music, there was no expectation for what I was doing, other than from myself. We just were both very peaceful and anxious to see what we would tap into. We had no idea what we would tap into until it started happening."

Ballard, for his part, agreed. "I didn't know anything about her and I don't think she knew anything about me. It was almost like we could leave all the baggage outside the door and approach it like we were just going to please ourselves. We don't think of ourselves, separately or collectively, as the sum of everything we've done. But I think when we got together, we said we're not going to play to any expectation other than our own. And I think that is a very liberating place to start. And it was a key. I didn't know what she wanted to do, we just kind of explored it together."

Once Morissette moved into Los Angeles to permit them more time to work together, they embarked on a system of trying out melodies on acoustic guitars, as well as exchanging ideas for lyrics. As well, because they were already collaborating in Ballard's home studio, they were able to record songs as they were written, sometimes overdubbing the contributions of other musicians.

"The more time we got to spend together, the deeper the connection for me, of understanding intellectually and emotionally where she was coming from," said Ballard. "Really it was more a matter of her getting deeper in what she wanted to say, and feeling the freedom to do it, finding an outlet for it." And Morissette, as is now well-known, was exploiting that outlet with tremendous verve, a veritable gusher of repressed anxieties and fears. "Finally I had this opportunity to be honest, in many ways for what seemed like the first time. A lot of it came out because I had been repressing it for so long," she said.

Ballard, too, was, if not escaping from repression, taking advantage of a new artistic freedom that perhaps he had denied himself over the years before he collaborated with Morissette. "I'm a facilitator of other people's artistic ambitions," he said afterwards. "I wasn't held down (in the past), but I wasn't using . . . all of the artistic judgment I could bring to something. Alanis certainly empowered me to be an artist with her, to say: Do your thing. We weren't trying to write for the market, so it was extremely liberating for me to have my creativity unleashed . . . I hadn't felt there was a situation for me to pour a lot of my music into."

Ballard also felt that the search for a new record deal for Morissette should be delayed until they were musically ready. "It was important from an artistic standpoint to keep control and not get a bunch of opinions until we were satisfied ourselves." As a result, by the time the pair had come up with an album's worth of material, they had no record contract. The next step was get the self-confessional frankness of JAGGED LITTLE PILL on record and before what would ultimately become apparent was an eagerly waiting audience.

SPIN
Alanis Morissette
Hot and Bothered
SPECIAL ISSUE
THE FUTURE
ROCK'N'ROLL
SEX FASHION
REBELLION DRUGS
AIDS CYBERSPACE
POLITICS AND DEATH
IN OUR LIFETIME
Guest Edited by JARON LANIER, Pioneer of VIRTUAL REALITY

GREEN DAY'S NEW ALBUM
Alanis Morissette
Angry White Female
SPECIAL REPORT
The Militias & the NRA
DAVID BOWIE & NINE INCH NAILS LIVE
BLUR
PRINCE
WILLIAM GREIDER
Clinton in a Funk
WHAT'S REALLY WRONG WITH AMERICA?
TRY YOUR PAYCHECK

·six·

Right Through You

I was just putting up with so much. I walk this fine line constantly of . . .
having respect and being diplomatic with people and then just standing up for myself, like where do you draw the line?

— *Alanis Morissette*

Hello Mr. Man
You didn't think I'd come back
You didn't think I'd show up with my army
And this ammunition on my back

— *Right Through You*

After Alanis Morissette and Glen Ballard achieved the freedom of creative expression they were seeking, they were faced with the next phase in the process of reaching their audience with their music, namely finding a record label which would appreciate the material that had gushed from their collaborative efforts in Ballard's studio. But they were faced with much more than that. While on the surface of it, finding an interested label was the practical step, the more profound issue remained grappling with the status quo which exists within the framework of the recording industry itself. There were a number of areas of potential conflict between the creators of the music who had exorcised their respective creative demons to compose songs they considered art, and the recording industry Establishment which tends to assess music less on the basis of art than on its potential for corporate profit.

The areas of potential conflict were and are much larger than specific songs or various recording companies themselves. At stake was the concept of artistic integrity itself, the anomaly of taking one's passionately conceived work and seeking the required corporate entity which would willingly convey that work to its potential audience. As is very often the case, the conflict arises out of two different views of the artistic endeavor itself. The artist's view is that something important has been said in the work of art and that there is an audience out there waiting to continue the dialogue the work of art inspires. The corporate entity's view, generally speaking, is that, while indeed all that artistic dialogue might be meaningful for artist and potential audience, it is not meaningful to the corporate entity until there is some assurance of economic profit. Worse yet, the apparent conflict in ideal has a corollary which can add further tension to the relationship, namely the tendency for the corporate entity to reserve the right to know better than the artist what is worthwhile product. The company tends to reinforce its claim to superior judgment under extremely rigid and narrow parameters. It tends to equate profitability of the product with its artistic value. If an artistic work doesn't make money, it can't be as good as the artist thinks it is.

But in Alanis Morissette's case, she was courting conflict in the area of an even larger and more pervasive issue. As a young woman, she was going to have to endure the various demonstrations of patronization, sexual objectification, and corporate good-old-boy-ism which continue to stand in the way of many women's honest artistic labors, regardless of whether it is rock music or another form of art. All artists must endure the profit versus art conflict. All female artists, even at this stage of the world's history, must also endure the additional resistance inherent in the fact they are women, that on a good day, the best they can expect is some polite condescension from the male power brokers who cling, tooth and nail, to their level of corporate influence.

Ultimately, the hunt for a satisfactory label arrived at a successful conclusion. "Four labels were interested in Morissette to varying degrees," Paul Cantin reported in the *Ottawa Sun*. "Maverick, a label set up especially for Madonna as part of her contract with Warner, was among the front-runners. Morissette's lawyer asked his partner to pass on a tape of the songs to his client, Guy Oseary, Maverick's A&R rep. Oseary 'flipped,' but the label wouldn't commit until they saw Morissette perform, so Welch set up a mini-concert for a small group of label executives, in Ballard's studio."

Welch said, "Glen played acoustic and she sang right there in front of them. Then they put the tape up and she went into the booth and sang one of the tracks. After about a half-hour they said: 'That's enough. Let's go outside.' And we basically made the deal in the hallway."

But if that makes it sound easy, it wasn't. In the period before the deal was struck with Maverick, Morissette was faced over and over again with frustrations based on her commitment to artistic integrity and the simple fact she was a young woman. "There's a bit of the old-school mentality. Not only was it difficult being chronologically young, but it was also being female . . . There are cases where the old-school mentality came into play, also the fact they were much older than I was. Their respect for art is very low on their priority list. Their very sort of money-hungry corporate way of thinking did not mesh at all with my purist, artistic outlook. (Meeting with labels) was very frustrating. I would come home from a lot of meetings and my manager would just sort of shake his head and put his arms around me and go: 'It's okay.' I was just putting up with so much. I walk this fine line constantly of, like, having respect and being diplomatic with people and then just standing up for myself, like where do you draw the line? It is a difficult position to be in, but I dealt with it in *Right Through You* in about ten minutes," she said.

Right Through You, with the often quoted lyric "You took a long hard look at my ass / And then played golf for a while," and Morissette's reference to herself as "Miss Thing," is much more than a slightly retaliatory look at corporate record label executives for objectifying the artist and her work, however. It becomes, in view of the feminist forces at work in rock music, a kind of blunt admission that in rock 'n' roll music there is a feminist rebellion underway.

In the way other songs on JAGGED LITTLE PILL would become anthems to psychological healing, self-awareness, and self-empowerment, and freedom from status quo repression, *Right Through You* would become an anthem in its own right, bluntly announcing the "army" and the "ammunition" behind the post-power feminist movement in rock music. In the year or more since the first indication of the fact that Morissette and JAGGED LITTLE PILL were going to be a phenomenon, the clairvoyance in Morissette's lyrics have resounded in the music industry and elsewhere more and more. There is not only a powerful female movement in rock, but it is powerfully feminist, embracing two main feminist approaches, but it also threatens, for the time being, to reduce men to secondary importance as rock 'n' roll artists themselves.

"An estro-wave of women artists has rendered the big-haired male rocker commercially impotent," boasts a sub-headline to an article in *The Globe and Mail* in January 1997 by Elizabeth Renzetti. "Celine Dion, the twitchy queen of the power ballad, has just been nominated for four Grammy Awards. Alanis Morissette, the Ottawa native whose fame sprang from pointed lyrics and a nasty mouth, is nominated for two Grammys for a song off her 1995 record JAGGED LITTLE PILL, the Energizer Bunny of the music charts," she wrote. "The two would seem to have little in common, apart from being Canadian and producing some of last year's top-selling records. There is also the little matter of their chromosomes: two Xs, count 'em.

"Those little Xs are marking the hottest ticket in pop music these days: the sound created by women, alone and in bands. Mention her sex to a performer and she's likely to punch you in the nose and yell about rock's proud 'herstory,' about Patti Smith and the Runaways and Joan Armatrading, but that doesn't change the fact that never has so much been sold by so many women. And it's not just rock music: There's an equally strong surge on the distaff side of country, middle-of-the road adult contemporary and hip hop." Renzetti backs up her view with a comment from David Farrell, publisher of Canada's trade music journal, *The Record*. "The big-haired, stereotypical male rocker has become impotent as a commercial entity. He's a yawn, a bore. The urgency or stridency of the message women are imparting is ringing a more urgent chord with audiences than the drivel that other rock stars have been producing."

The basic focus of Renzetti's remarks offers a kind of statistical evidence that female musicians are taking their place in their music genres, especially as performers, although Renzetti also points out the corporate echelons of music are still manned by the male old guard. But the statistical evidence has a tendency to enter the discussion after the fact. The key issue is not that audience recognition of female music has drastically increased in the past decade, but that it is because the performers are saying something to which the audience can respond. Renzetti's assessment, like others similar in observation, has a tendency to gauge the female success by the amount of male success it has displaced, as if to say it's sunny outside because it is no longer raining, rather than simply to marvel at the sunshine itself.

"It's self-evident that the path of women in music is the same one broken by women in Western society as a whole: a gradual pattern of gaining control," she says. This view tends to discredit the earlier representatives of the women's movement in rock music, disparages any kind of feminism except power feminism, and doesn't consider that the audience's new appreciation for female-produced music demonstrates the quality of the music more than any statistical inquiry into how many females have displaced how many males. Morissette, for instance, has sold in excess of 15 million copies of JAGGED LITTLE PILL less because she has maintained control of her musical career but more because she's conveyed an honesty to an audience prepared to listen.

Morissette's "army" in *Right Through You* is all the female rockers touching a nerve with music audiences these days. Her "ammunition" is what she and her peers are musically conveying. Ironically, with so many males still controlling the top levels of the corporate musical echelon, the statistics are *their* domain and *their* justification for the feminist movement in music; it's taking the art of the music and reducing it to a coldly pragmatic matter of dollars and cents. And that's why males aren't communicating with their audiences as well these days. To see the trend as evidence of female performers supplanting males is to miss the point.

The real power in this new feminist march in music is not that it takes out the males, but that it forces them to acknowledge their art and, more importantly, that their audience is willing to pay top dollar for that art. When Morissette refers to herself as "Miss Thing," she is not gloating over her role in a successful trend of female rockers supplanting male rockers, but impressing upon her audience that the rigid and narrow male domain in the upper reaches of rock production was at times unable to recognize her appeal to that same audience, an appeal by the way based on ability and the art itself, not on which sex she represents.

In a broader sense, there have always been two directions which feminism could choose to take. There have been issues of sexual objectification and oppression which a fair-minded society must bring to a necessary termination, the way it must conclude *all* types of oppression. And there has been a feminism which seeks to remove the male power brokers and replace them with female power brokers, presumably as a first step towards achieving the other option. The idea of this latter route to power is that, with power, comes the influence to make positive and just changes. Interestingly enough, rock music has always seemed to blend both routes somehow, but with a slight preference for the identifying oppression option and expressing an outrage over its existence.

Rock music is the perfect medium for addressing these issues. Even in this decade, music and other performing arts continue to insist in some quarters that women adhere to a male-dominated definition of glamor and worth. Morissette has often related how, as a younger woman, a teenager, there was an emphasis placed on her décolletage as opposed to the artistic message she was trying to convey in her music. In some genres, this quest for stereotypical glamor among females artists even tampers with their natural bodies. Women are encouraged, through plastic surgery and other "medical" procedures, to change the shape of their hips, their breasts, and other aspects of their physical appearance, these days prevalently in the genre of country music. Even where such drastic measures are not suggested, there is a focus placed on thinness and other glamorous preoccupations which tend to reinforce a male stereotype of what a female singer, actor, or other kind of performer should look like, as a prerequisite to a successful career.

Books have been written expressing the depth of this problem and the outrage many women feel about it. Susan Faludi's *Backlash*, for example, addresses this issue, in the context of the continuing attempt by a worldwide male dominated corporate structure to insist on this stereotype and creating a backlash against feminism as one major means of doing so. Not only does this backlash tend to objectify women but it has also been necessary at the corporate level to ensure profits for commodities such as cosmetics. Although Faludi and others with a similar point to make are focusing on the backlash and on stereotyping women for gain and for power, they also reflect a more broad call for justice where *anyone* is a victim of oppression. For some time now, an entire branch of feminism has realized quite accurately that women are not only oppressed because they are women but because a broader state of oppression actually exists, an oppressive mentality, if you will, which victimizes other groups, minorities, and individuals.

But, as mentioned, there is another school of feminist thought, promoted by writers such as Naomi Wolf in books like *Fire With Fire*. The basic premise of this school is that women cannot escape their oppression until they assume power over their current oppressors. And they cannot do that without playing the power games which will place them in a position to do so. In other words, the end will justify the means. Once women have assumed control of the various corporate boardrooms, by matching their male counterparts stride for stride in a vicious race to power, they can then free themselves of oppression. What this strategy fails to consider, however, is that to reach the top in a way which duplicates male power achievement, women must therefore duplicate the activities of their male counterparts with respect to other areas of oppression. The actual war against oppression of every kind becomes supplanted by the war against oppression against women instead. In the end there becomes a very real possibility that other kinds of oppression remain after women have achieved their goals and all that has changed is the gender of the power broker.

The phenomenon of the growing number of female rock and pop superstars, however, has a tendency to reflect the possibly unnecessary rewards of the quest to head into the boardroom. Female musical stars, of which Morissette is now the predominant member, are now discovering that they can voice their outrage, not only as women and feminists, but as human beings violated by other status quo tyrannies as well. Not only can they say their piece on their own terms, within the context of creative artistic integrity, but they can do so before an ever-increasing audience which responds to the message in their lyrics. Ironically, this ultimately achieves the same end as the power competition approach. It forces the male-dominated recording industry, even as it uses its own narrow criteria of profit and economics as a measuring stick, to promote the message the women artists wish to relate, because it is profitable to do so. This, in turn, only serves to further increase the size of the audience.

Even more importantly, the tremendous response female artists such as Morissette are achieving in front of their audiences demonstrates that the reception to the message is there and growing. This means the victims of a wide variety of oppressive social attitudes can be galvanized until, potentially and ideally, the very concept of oppression itself is repeatedly examined as something the people on this planet should rise above. Be it economic, environmental, political, violent, psychological, or artistic tyranny, the framework is there to attack them all. In the arena of rock music, it would appear that the rising multitude of successful female artists has become aware that when everyone on this planet is guaranteed their basic rights, the "everyone" in question will include women. If no one is stereotyped, denied opportunity, objectified, prevented from expressing themselves creatively, or psychologically repressed by a societal status quo, then women will not be treated that way either.

Several of Alanis Morissette's songs on JAGGED LITTLE PILL may express outrage over corporate record executives and their male-dominated objectification of women and the young, but it also expresses a broader range of both outrage and personal hope, as she sings, for example, in *Hand In My Pocket*:

> I'm broke but I'm happy
> I'm poor but I'm kind
> I'm short but I'm healthy, yeah
> I'm high but I'm grounded
> I'm sane but I'm overwhelmed
> I'm lost but I'm hopeful baby
>
> — *Hand In My Pocket*

This song, in particular, has become an anthem for her audiences, the suggestion it makes that there is an alternative to the injustices which oppress all of us, and that the alternative is in achieving a personal balance, not giving up, regardless of which creative vision we have inside us and regardless of the societal obstacles placed before us.

As has already been pointed out, rock music has a history as a genre of taking on the Establishment. It has done so, however, within the texture of its art primarily, less in the corporate record label boardrooms. These latter paragon shelters have a tendency to react to trends on the basis of economics. The artists, however, are more proactive, doggedly keeping the faith that they can convey the honesty in their music despite the music industry's compliance in music mass delivery. As Renzetti put it, "If women are making a splash on the charts, it's not because their sisters have taken over the boardrooms."

No, it's because the sisters have something important to say. And, for that reason, because it is important, an ever-accelerating larger audience is listening. And that audience isn't caring about glamor, surgically improved body parts, or a preconceived notion of femininity — whether glamor surrounds the performer or not. Instead, the audience is hearing the message of self-empowerment and the ensuing outrage that should be expressed when that self-empowerment is impeded. And if these performers paint their nails, what impact does it have on the message in their music? Apparently none. It may not be classic feminism, but it's feminism just the same. And it's rock music, too. Because it's shaking up the Establishment again, as rock rebellion has always been wont to do.

Having maintained that there is a legitimate movement going on in rock music these days, that women are leading that movement through a frank approach to their art and discussion in their lyrics of a series of broad societal issues, and that audiences, regardless of their gender, are finding something meaningful in what these women are saying, the inevitable word of caution stumbles inexorably into the picture. It's that peculiar "age of irony" disease that translates as "uncool" any initiative which, a moment before, has been pronounced "cool." It's that fear that something which is, in the strict meaning of the word, a trend, that is a cultural development, will be tagged a "trend" and will, accordingly become a bullet from which all the gunpowder has been removed.

One of the most powerful factors in this, the age of irony, is the impact of the news media on an entire generation. The news media, generally speaking, committed to analyzing trends, trying self-indulgently to anticipate them, transforming all cultural developments into something superficial and vacuous, is a powerful force in the cynicism of the age of irony. Each time there is a legitimate movement about to begin, the media gets hold of it, shoots if full of superficial holes, reduces it to economic analysis, pulls an unwilling group of fringe players into the discussion, and ultimately empties the movement of any influence by trivializing it. Pronouncing it a trend, the media diffuses any real alternative in the movement by absorbing its superficialities into the mainstream of the status quo.

The news media has significantly changed in the past 30 years. Thirty years is long enough for there to be a new generation which can be manipulated by the still relatively new journalistic focus on superficiality. The vast array of "puff" stories, entertainment profiles, televised interviews without any meat, comparisons, trend reports, and other fatuous reportage tend to make even the most significant cultural development look like some passing phase. This approach to the serious business of culture, and its coincidental and willful act of ignoring social issues as perceived by the cultural performing mirror often held up to them for examination, not only inspires a sense of cynicism in an entire generation, but, at the same time, waters and fertilizes it. In the case of legitimately silly trends such as pet rocks, there is no harm done. But when art focuses its gaze and compassion on more serious human issues such as oppression, abuse, feminism, psychological health, and much more, there is a void of communication put in place and sustained which equates important issues with true trends. The void tends to leave an entire generation not believing in the existence of oppression in the same way they don't believe in a pet rock.

There are forces which wish to resist any change in this situation. The news media is the voice of the corporate giant, the same corporate giant with which earnest young musicians must deal when it comes to having their art reach a large audience. There is not a large and well sustained independent media voice in most countries in western civilization any longer. Instead, there is this corporate media giant owned by a handful of powerful barons committed to a course of non-communication designed to trivialize and diffuse any serious cultural movement towards change. It is to this corporate media's advantage to create and sustain an entire generation so cynical it no longer believes there can be a true alternative to the state of disenfranchisement they suffer at this point in history. The advantage to the media is that such a generation presents no challenge or threat to the status quo, will meekly succumb to current economic-political fashion because it has no faith that any significant portent of change is anything more than an empty trend.

The danger, where performers such as Alanis Morissette and her female peers are concerned, is that the thrust of their message will get lost when media analysis of their popularity diffuses the importance of the reasons for that popularity. The meat in the lyrics and the motivation behind the outrage disappear in the resulting vacuum. Tags such as "angry women of rock" have a tendency to objectify important cultural statements as the popular rantings of performers who are, because they've been identified as a trend, already on their way out.

Several months ago, Morissette autographed for a fan in New York a daily newspaper article written about her, prior to performing. "Don't believe everything you read," she told the fan.

She wasn't talking about statistical data, record sales, the date of her performance, the location of the concert. She was talking about the more subtle material which works its way into the stories, the tags which dismiss what she is saying, the allusions to passing trend, the subtle manipulations in the media that trivialize her and other female musicians' phenomenal popularity with audiences, even while it reports that popularity.

Examples abound. Elizabeth Renzetti's *Globe and Mail* article contains such fare, not only directly, but alluding to other similar reports. "There's a particular kind of lush, middle-of-the-road balladry that radio has always found non-threatening and embraced, from Carly Simon until today's leading chanteuses, [Celine] Dion and Mariah Carey and Whitney Houston. Now the margins are paved with gold as well and radio programmers warm to the unlikely yowlings of Iceland's Bjork and Dolores O'Riordan from the Cranberries. Sarah McLachlan of Vancouver took the theory of female bonding to a more lucrative plane in the fall of last year with her all-woman Lilith Fair, a tour featuring McLachlan, Lisa Loeb, Emmylou Harris and others. Another tour is planned for this summer with an even higher-profile roster, including Bjork, Nenah Cherry and Tori Amos. (It's a sign of just how far we haven't come that the first tour was dubbed Vulvapalooza in *Rolling Stone* magazine and a headline in the L.A.

Times read: 'Sara McLachlan getting even with the guys.')"

Although there is an element of truth in the fact that the success of Morissette's JAGGED LITTLE PILL has made it easier economically for other female artists to get their chance to communicate with a larger audience, this fact is moderated by the defining-it-as-trend factor and by its tendency to dismiss new artists as copies of Morissette and other popular performers, as well as by media attempts to insinuate conflict in a purported competition between the artists. Says Renzetti, for example, "The women producing that deeply personal music continue to be snapped up by record companies in the wake of the international success of that blessed Canadian trinity, Dion, Morissette and new-country poster girl Shania Twain. A whole estrowave of young artists is being dragged along on their trains: Kim Stockwood, Chantal Keviazuk, Kinnie Starr and Amanda Marshall here in Canada. Jewel and Tracy Bonham and Fiona Apple south of the border."

Even articles which focus on other artists have a tendency to do so mainly from the standpoint of comparison with Morissette, not from the point of view of the message they are transmitting and its function in a possible movement, but in a competitive, divide-and-conquer sense. The sub-headline in a *Toronto Sun* article by Jane Stevenson about Tracy Bonham in March of 1996 claimed, "Singer Battles Comparisons with Alanis Morissette." Not only did this approach trivialize the work of Morissette, but it trivialized the work of Bonham and the coalescing forces which make these performers part of a larger and much more important movement.

"Tracy Bonham's major-label debut is called *The Burdens Of Being Upright*, but it might as well be called The Burdens Of Being Called The Next Alanis Morissette. Like every current female singer who's not afraid to spill her guts musically, the fast-rising Boston singer-songwriter has been lumped in with the Ottawa-Born, L.A.-based Morissette," wrote Stevenson. The key words are "every current female singer who's not afraid to spill her guts musically," as demonstrative of the trend, the implication being that it is just a trend. Never mind what it says to diffuse Bonham's music and the message in her lyrics to which, apparently, audiences are also responding. Stevenson goes even further to imply that Bonham is legitimately concerned about the comparison when, in fact, she is probably *tired* of the *media* comparison.

"There was one gig in Ottawa where I had to stop and say something 'cause I felt I was turning into her," said Bonham in the Stevenson article, "because people were looking at me as if I was her. And I had this weird sensation of like, 'Oh, my God. All of a sudden I sound like her and I'm acting like her.' All I know is that we're both female. People are just quick to judge or something. It's weird. When I first heard that, I laughed. It doesn't make sense to me at all."

Stevenson also takes the liberty of suggesting that "the biggest difference between Morissette and Bonham may be that Bonham actually speaks to Canadian reporters. In fact she apologized for cancelling an interview when she was in town earlier because she had a cold. She was also upset at a Toronto article that suggested she was being strategically groomed to be the next Morissette. During her Toronto performance, she lambasted the article's author as 'one of the most shallow rock critics' she had ever met." Bonham may later learn what Morissette apparently already knows, that too much talking to the media at the wrong time can sometimes undermine everything you're trying to accomplish artistically.

Stevenson takes a similar approach of superficial trendiness in an August 1996 article, "Pop Queens Reign as Cover Girls," in the *Toronto Sun*. "Check out the magazines stands this week and you'll see Canada's most successful female pop singers in the world staring back at you," wrote Stevenson. "Quebec's ultra-polished Celine Dion, fresh off her Olympics opening ceremony performance, has scored a major coup by appearing on the Aug. 12 cover of *Time Magazine*. The more aggressively-inclined Alanis Morissette, who's named in the *Time* article as 'the outlaw diva or anti-diva,' peers out from the cover of this months British *Q* magazine obscured by the headline: 'Young, sexy, talented and bloody popular!'" From there it's a bit of a report on who sold the most seats in a specific concert location, who has sold the most albums and why and even an anecdote about some stolen tapes in Washington State. Beyond that, the article anticipates Morissette breaking the world record of best-selling female album ever, then held by Whitney Houston in 1985. "Frankly," comments Stevenson, "anyone who can dethrone Houston is okay by me." If you want to trivialize everyone's music, you can set them up as being in musical and album-selling competition.

"Women Artists Dealing With The Shadow of Morissette," proclaims the headline in an article by David Bauder of the Associated Press in August of 1996. "Alanis Morissette. Alanis Morissette. Alanis Morissette. There. Most women rock artists who emerged in the months after *You Oughta Know* already expect to hear that name mentioned in connection with their careers, it's best to get it out of the way early," wrote Bauder. "Morissette has become such a phenomenon in one year that her legacy represents both an opportunity and burden for many singers. Tracy Bonham and Patti Rothberg are two cases in point. On the one hand, the music industry's follow-the-leader devotion to trends means it's a good time to be a young female songwriter, particularly one who writes bluntly about life experiences. Yet, it also can be difficult for such a writer to establish her own identity and fight through the suspicion that she's taken cues from Morissette, even with marked differences in style and outlook. If there's one thing that makes Bonham particularly angry, it's being lumped in with a supposed movement of 'angry young females.'"

"It's so ignorant and shallow," Bonham is reported to have told *Billboard*. "It's an ongoing thing, and I constantly have to defend myself. People would think that I'm angry just because they hear me scream. They obviously didn't listen well. People just don't know how to handle it if a woman uses smarts and brains."

Unable to nail down any indication that Bonham has a legitimate problem with Morissette, Bauder slips into a vague allusion to competition and discord anyway. "Actually," he wrote, "she does slyly take a peer to task on her debut album, but it's Courtney Love and not Morissette. Bonham . . . has described *Kisses* as a song about a performer who tries to make a spectacle of herself." Details beyond this circumstantial bit of information are not included in the article.

With respect to Rothberg, Bauder maintains the comparisons

with Morissette may come from a song entitled *This One's Mine* in which she "revels in revenge" with the lyric "I could say that you were a dirty dog but that's an insult to the fleas." But he also reports that Rothberg was impressed when she first saw the video to Morissette's *You Oughta Know*. "I was like, 'Wow. Who's this girl?' I was totally supportive of it," said Rothberg.

Perhaps more clearly indicative of the movement in today's rock and pop music towards an honest and more prevalent female voice and how it so far has resisted media attempts to turn it into a shallow trend was demonstrated during the Grammy Awards telecast in early 1996 when Annie Lennox, while receiving her Grammy during an evening where men might just have well stayed home, clearly expressed her pleasure that so many women were being honored with awards and producing great work. There was no spirit of empty competition in her voice, and she spoke with the calm assurance of someone not surprised by this development. If it has been declared just the latest in a string of popular culture trends which come and go, it was not apparent that Annie Lennox thought so. Nor was it in Alanis Morissette's mind when she rose to pay tribute to Lennox as she stood on stage, receiving *her* award.

The main point here is that the audience has shown itself to be the determining factor in this movement of honest, sometimes brutally candid music emanating from the pens of a sex which, because of its own oppression, is more intimately aware of the ills being perpetuated in this dark era of world history in which so many victims suffer oppression. The audience is responding to the message, not because there is a trend being manipulated here by power broker record execs, but because the coalescing of more powerful, blunt lyrics with a large audience willing to share in the message within those lyrics is leaving those executives little choice, based on their own economic definition of what should be produced, their own "meal ticket taste," to use Morissette's words in *Right Through You*.

A further look at the female artists, both past and present, who comprise this movement only demonstrates that it is an artistic and ultimately political movement which has found an ideal audience in this age of irony. It remains to be seen, however, whether continued media (corporate) or music executive (corporate) forces, in their zeal to define all human experience on the basis of the free market only, can successfully diffuse the rather moving and distinctly encouraging relationship which is developing between female performers and an audience eager to listen to what they say.

·seven·

You Oughta Know

I played the record [Tori Amos's LITTLE EARTH-QUAKES] in its entirety, lying on my living room floor, and I just bawled my eyes out. . . . I was so grateful.

— *Alanis Morissette*

You seem very well, things look peaceful
I'm not quite as well, I thought you should know

— *You Oughta Know*

If one wants to find a true indication that there is, indeed, a women's movement in contemporary pop and rock music, one can temporarily set aside the reams of material being written about the subject and study, instead, an average music chart in an average small town in, say, Canada. One might look, for instance, at the 1996 top 100 songs as published by 1380 CKLC in Kingston, Ontario, Canada, in the January 4, 1997 issue of local daily newspaper, *The Whig-Standard.* On this chart, Alanis Morissette appears as number one with *Ironic*; in fact, Morissette also has the number six spot with *You Learn,* number 53 with *Head Over Feet,* and number 56 with *Hand In My Pocket.* But it isn't just Morissette. Number two is *Give Me One Reason* by Tracy Chapman, number 3 *Because You Loved Me* by Celine Dion, number 4 *I Love You Always Forever* by Donna Lewis, and number 5 *One Of Us* by Joan Osborne. And so it goes, including other songs by some of these same artists, plus high ranking singles by Amanda Marshall, Melissa Etheridge, Sheryl Crow, and Kim Stockwood.

In blunt terms, record company bigwigs can term the female boom a trend if they want to before hopping on for the ride, but to do so does not ensure the kind of public audience response that female artists are now receiving. No, it's exactly the other way around. In a statement, female artists, who have always been arguably in the forefront of creating musical material which reflects artistic and social outrage, are now getting their voice because someone wants to hear it. It's the record business itself which is still locked in the shallow puddle of trend, trying desperately to understand the ocean of response which Morissette and her peers have unleashed.

As JAGGED LITTLE PILL, almost from the moment it was released, raced up the *Billboard* charts, then stayed there, apparently forever, record producers described its success rate as "scary." At the very least, scary is a vague admission that something puzzling is going on. And the record companies have been trying to catch up ever since. Yet as Terry McBride, Vancouver-based manager for Sarah McLachlan explained in January 1997 during an interview by Lynn Saxberg in the *Toronto Star,* "I don't really think it was a breakthrough year. The simple fact is that everyone's waking up to it because the public's buying the records.

It's just like a snowball going downhill. It's getting bigger." McBride is right. The message has always been there, but it's the audience which is changing. Regardless of gender, what has been released is an audience seeking some honest outrage and change in its rock music. And whether the status quo likes it or not, whether they are even able to understand it or not, there's a rebellion in the wind against the sanitized conservatism the status quo utilizes to obscure its dirty laundry. So the analysis just goes on and the female artists in question continue to express their bemusement over the fact that people are waking up to something which has been in place much longer than it appears.

Saxberg, writing about the phenomenon as a trend and focusing primarily on the Canadian component of that trend, talks with three of the less well-known Canadian members of the movement, but quickly rising musical stars in their own right, Amanda Marshall, Kim Stockwood, and Wendy Lands. Marshall, for example, is bemused at world reaction to the phenomenon. "Everyone asks me, 'What is going on with Canadian women? What the hell is in the water up there?' . . . The people who are getting all the attention now, including myself, have been working much longer than people have been aware of us. (The attention) is very nice but I don't think we all feel like we've joined this club."

Lands, who released ANGELS AND ORDINARY MEN in 1996, added, "When I was a kid, I didn't grow up wanting to be a female artist. I grew up wanting to be an artist. I do feel like people are clumping me into the Canadian female singer / songwriter thing and I wonder, do they do that to men, too?" Stockwood, whose song *Jerk* with the unforgettable (for a man, at least) refrain "You jerk, you jerk, you are such a jerk," says this kind of development has been in the making for some time. "I just think it's about time. I don't think women have got more vocal because we've been vocal for a long time, but it just so happens it's happening now and that's incredible." Prince Edward Island native Tara MacLean alludes to "women smashing through with gentle passion. People are needing to hear something in their hearts now. We've been cut off for a long time and people are getting back in touch with their emotions. I think that the women out there are really touching that. Everyone is wanting to feel things."

Saxberg, herself, admits "Canadian women have long been forging their own paths in music" because they are "articulate, talented and unique in style. . . . From the ground-breaking folk songs of Joni Mitchell and Buffy Sainte-Marie in the 1960s to k.d. lang and Sarah McLachlan in the '90s, the country has had a strong tradition of women who express their emotions in songs that are a little off the beaten track, but still hit a nerve in mainstream listeners."

An issue of *Time* magazine in August of 1996 took a look at this women's music movement, declaring, "With lush ballads and some amazing vocal virtuosity, women singers are upending the old bad-boy world of popular music." But in the piece writer Richard Corliss added "cynics would say a miracle of marketing by canny record executives" when he tried to come up with a reason for the movement. It's a point of view which somehow insults the audience, the other partner in the outrage manifesto that is going on out there. Audiences aren't nearly as malleable as writers like Corliss or record executives would have us believe.

Even when *People* magazine studied the issue in a March 1996 article, the sense of puzzlement dotted every "i" and crossed every "t". "Something's happening here, though what it is ain't exactly clear," reported *People*. "Last month, when announcing the nominees for the Grammy Awards, a spokesman heralded the ascendancy of females in rock's traditionally male domain by declaring, 'This is the year of the woman.' If so, why now?" Most of *People*'s response was, at best, speculative and cynical and did not take into consideration the history of female outrage, so lost was it in the immediacy of the present "trend." "Because 'male rock is running into cliches and self-parody,' Lucy O'Brien, author of *SheBop: The Definitive History of Women in Rock, Pop & Soul*, offers as an explanation. Laura Lee Davies, music editor of the British magazine *Time Out*, agrees that some guy-rock can seem stale, especially in comparison to, say, Alanis Morissette and PJ Harvey, quirky performers who have hit the mainstream with their over-the-top personas intact. 'Women are better at playing around with image,' says Davies. 'Boys still get a bit self-conscious if they try anything more than putting on a checkered shirt and standing behind a guitar.' And, of course, this being rock and roll, it's all probably somehow related to sex. Many of the women nominees are startlingly forthright about matters sexual. 'That part of rock has been really boring in the last few years,' says Geffen Records vice-president Robin Sloane. 'Women see the world differently.' Female musicians, she says, are 'the most exciting thing happening.'''

In truth, with respect to attempts to reach out to a caring, compassionate audience, female musicians have been exciting for nearly three decades. And although the audience has shown glimmers of embracing that excitement, it is now determined to share the emotional outrage of rock's female performers in ways in which it has previously been unwilling. The evidence of the intensity of the movement and the fact that it has a history are plain to see. The history of the movement not only perhaps explains Alanis Morissette's startling success with JAGGED LITTLE PILL, but points out, in a broader way, the inevitability of that success.

As has been mentioned already, two of the leading influences on women's music also come from Canada, Buffy Sainte-Marie and Joni Mitchell. Sainte-Marie is the most famous Native American artist in popular music. Hailing from Saskatchewan, born of Cree Indian parents, she has continued to produce albums in the 1990s, music which has not only focused attention on native issues but on the ever-growing gap between rich and poor in North America. Joni Mitchell is now a musical legend, whose music Alanis Morissette grew up with in her parents' home in Ottawa and to which, in recent years, she has begun to listen to again.

Mitchell has commanded a large, loyal following of dedicated fans over the years, people who already know that her particular voice of outrage has a gift for accurately addressing a wide variety of social issues. Combined with a willingness to experiment with various styles of music, Mitchell has puzzled music critics over the years. "One of the most respected singer/songwriters in rock, Joni Mitchell is also one of its most daring and uncompromising innovators," says *The New Rolling Stone Encyclopedia of Rock & Roll*. "Her career has ranged from late-Sixties and early-Seventies popularity with confessional folk-pop songs to her current cult status via a series of jazz-inflected works that presaged the multicultural and world-music experiments of Paul Simon, Peter Gabriel, and Sting by more than a decade. Through the Eighties and Nineties, Mitchell's influence could be seen in a range of artists, from contemporary confessional singer/songwriters to Prince."

Born Roberta Joan Anderson in 1943 in Fort MacLeod, she grew up in Saskatoon. After being stricken with polio at age nine, she defied medical predictions that she would never walk and recovered. She taught herself to play guitar from a Pete Seeger instruction book and began to play folk music after she enrolled at the Alberta College of Art in Calgary. Not long afterwards, she moved to Toronto and began to perform in the burgeoning folk scene there, then married folksinger Chuck Mitchell, whom she divorced not long after moving to Detroit. After a series of successful engagements in New York, she signed a recording contract with a major label in 1968. Numerous other artists recorded her work preliminary to her own recording of her music, which helped to establish her reputation.

Although Mitchell has had her share of platinum albums and successful singles — COURT AND SPARK remains her highest-charting album at number 2 — her popularity has revolved around a large and dedicated cult following which has stuck by her, regardless of the direction her music has taken. At all times, however, that music has been bluntly honest and has presaged the confessional and pointed lyrics of Alanis Morissette and her peers. By the time she recorded DOG EAT DOG in 1985, her work was moving more towards social commentary than personal introspection. She has also independently produced or co-produced each of her albums since her debut (which was produced by David Crosby), and as a painter and photographer, for which she is also world-renowned, Mitchell has created the art for her albums.

When you examine the lyrics of Joni Mitchell over the years, the link between her and the women expressing their outrage now is easily seen. Note the lyrics for *Not To Blame* from her album TURBULENT INDIGO, for example:

The story hit the news
From coast to coast.
They said you beat the girl
You loved the most.
Your charitable acts
Seemed out of place,
With the beauty
With your fist marks on her face.
— *Not To Blame*

Or *Come In From The Cold* on her 1991 album NIGHT RIDE HOME:

We really thought we had a purpose
We were so anxious to achieve
We had hope
The world held promise
For a slave
To liberty
Freely I slaved away for something better
And I was bought and sold
And all I ever wanted
Was to come in from the cold.
— *Come In From The Cold*

What establishes the connection so provocatively between Mitchell's work throughout her career and the women artists in the 1990s is that the focus on so-called women's issues translates itself into a focus on the oppression most of us suffer at the hands of a world concentrating power into privileged hands. Even religion does not escape Mitchell's wrath, as it has not escaped Morissette's complaints in her song *Forgiven* on JAGGED LITTLE PILL:

I sang Alleluia in the choir
I confessed my darkest deeds to an envious man

My brothers they never went blind for what they did
But I may as well have.

— *Forgiven*

This theme of repression of women at the hands of organized religion, specifically its failure to acknowledge normal female passion and love, shows up as well in Joni Mitchell's *The Magdalene Laundries:*

I was an unmarried girl
I'd just turned twenty-seven
When they sent me to the sisters
For the way men looked at me.

The song continues:

Most girls come here pregnant
Some by their own fathers.
Bridget got that belly
By her parish priest.

— *The Magdalene Laundries*

For anyone sensitive to the message in women's music, it was a profoundly rewarding coincidence during the 1996 Grammy Awards presentations to see Joni Mitchell receive another Grammy for her efforts on the same night when Alanis Morissette was walking to the podium to receive so much hardware for JAGGED LITTLE PILL. Not ironic at all. Instead, it was a kind of profound justice. And it was also an indication that what was once perceived as true by a so-called counter culture following is now perceived as true by a vast pop culture audience.

Alanis Morissette has also been studying the history of another example of that bridge between past and present, where female outrage is concerned and where the exploitation of female artists by the music industry itself has now created an assortment of artists who are going to speak their minds in retaliation. In a variety of media interviews, when asked what she reads, Morissette has not only confessed to her regular diet of psychologically-oriented reading material, but specifically has mentioned *Faithfull,* the autobiography of Marianne Faithfull, co-written with David Dalton. Faithfull may be one of the best examples of exploited womanhood in the music industry. Stories of management demanding incessant touring, drug abuse and her sexual abuse become representative examples of female outrage in the making. And Faithfull's notorious song *Why D'Ya Do It* is so blunt an evocation of romantic revenge, it makes Morissette's *You Oughta Know* pale in comparison.

The comparison has not gone unnoticed among some music journalists. Julene Snyder in *Bam* magazine in July 1995 found comparisons between the two songs and the shared outrage Faithfull and Morissette both inspire. "Taut as a length of cat-gut stretched to the breaking point, the recording of *You Oughta Know* enlists Dave Navarro on guitars and Flea on bass, but it's Morissette's genuine wrathful ache that makes the track soar," writes Snyder. "Like Marianne Faithfull's *Why D'Ya Do It,* the crude language and lust for revenge transcends one woman's experience to become heartbreak's new theme song."

Faithfull, born in London, England, in 1946, first came to musical prominence in 1964, at the age of 17, when she recorded a Mick Jagger-Keith Richards song, *As Tears Go By* (she later became Jagger's girlfriend until she broke up with him in 1970). This was followed by three other hit songs independent of the Rolling Stones. Faithfull gave up recording in 1966 for an acting career, but this career ended following a miscarriage and her commitment to hospital to cure her heroin addiction (she contributed lyrics to the Stones' song *Sister Morphine).*

"Faithfull withdrew from public life, reappearing only briefly in 1974 on a David Bowie television special," reports *The New Rolling Stone Encyclopedia of Rock & Roll.* "In 1977 she recorded her first album in over ten years, and although it received little notice, it led to her signing with Island Records in 1979. Her Island debut, BROKEN ENGLISH, marked by stark instrumentation, venomous lyrics, and Faithfull's raspy vocals, was barely recognizable as the work of the woman who sang *As Tears Go By.* It was followed by several more critically acclaimed albums for Island." Britain has also produced the powerful Kate Bush, who, if not acknowledged to be an influence on Alanis Morissette, is at least an influence on the work of Morissette's peers such as Sinead O'Connor, Jane Siberry, Bjork, Tori Amos, and Dolores O'Riordan of the Cranberries. Described as idiosyncratic, Bush is a music critics favorite who records in her own home, directs her own videos, and combines a wide variety of musical influences, as well as literature, to create a more artistic plane for her music. Her tremendous vocal range and theatrical approach has inspired modern female rockers to explore a wide range of emotional presentation in their music, an emotional approach which reinforces the power in their lyrics.

Bush, who was born in 1958, is considered an art-rock prodigy. "She had been writing songs for two years when family friends told Dave Gilmour of Pink Floyd about the 16-year old's four-octave range and interest in the supernatural," reports *Rolling Stone*. "Gilmour financed the demo tape that got her signed to EMI. Because of her age and developing talent, she spent the next two years studying music, dance, and mime and writing the songs for her first album, recorded in 1977 under the supervision of Gilmour and producer Andrew Powell (Pink Floyd, Alan Parsons, Cockney Rebel). The album was preceded by the release of *Wuthering Heights*. The song's runaway success also spurred sales of the Emily Bronte novel."

The source of Bush's inspiration to various female artists this decade is the independence with which she approaches her work, the artistic control she holds over the production, often using the recording studio as an instrument itself, and her willingness to break new musical ground to build a structure for her darkly romantic literary lyrics. Although she approaches female and social issues from a more refined, artistic point of view, she nonetheless is considered a powerful voice in the background of today's more intense expression of the female experience.

Patti Smith, an American contemporary, likewise brought a literary intelligence to her lyrics but charged her music with a punk sound and attitude. Her brilliant cover of The Who's 1960s anthem *My Generation* on her album HORSES became an anthem for the 1970s punk generation. She is even credited with releasing what some consider the first punk-rock record, an independent 1974 single *Hey Joe* and *Piss Factory*. Smith is also a published poet with books such as *Babel*, *Seventh Heaven*, *Witt*, and *Kodak* to her credit, and co-author with Sam Shepard of the the play, *Cowboy Mouth*. In the 1970s punk-poet Smith claimed what *Rolling Stone* termed "the rock-musician-as-shaman role previously reserved by males." Compared to Jim Morrison, she has sometimes presented herself as well as a voice of rebellion, not only on behalf of women but with respect to victims generally, especially in such songs as *People Have The Power* on her 1988 album DREAM OF LIFE. Reportedly mellowed by motherhood, Smith nonetheless remains a powerful force in music and an uncompromising component in the current appreciation audiences have for what women are saying.

Alanis Morissette, however, is a nineties artist and much of what has influenced her seems to be the work of her decade's peers. Cited specifically is the work of Tori Amos. In fact, Morissette has maintained that Amos' album LITTLE EARTHQUAKES had a cathartic effect on her. "I played the record in its entirety, lying on my living room floor, and I just bawled my eyes out," she told *Q* magazine. "I was so grateful." The connection makes a great deal of sense from the standpoint that both artists deal explicitly with what has brought them to this point in their lives — and in a blunt fashion.

Amos, like Kate Bush, has for much of her career been identified as a child prodigy. She began tinkering on the piano at the age of two and a half, and by five was studying classical piano at the Peabody Institute at John Hopkins University in Baltimore. Her scholarship was not renewed when she insisted on performing her own pop compositions before the school's examination board. After a rough start attempting to become a successful rock musician, she released LITTLE EARTHQUAKES in 1992, which included the well-known song *Me And A Gun*, an autobiographical treatment of her rape by an acquaintance.

Amos, more than anything, wants to be brutally honest. She is uncompromising in her intention to blend artistic integrity with her experiences as a woman. Discussing *Me And A Gun* in *Hot Press* magazine, she said, "Any man who gets killed raping someone (such as in the movie, *Thelma and Louise*) has crossed the line. But I didn't kill him. I finally wrote a song about it instead and that has given me the freedom. *Me And A Gun* is not about him. It's more about me forgiving myself. That's why my music now is so therapeutic, so cathartic for me. I made a commitment not to be a victim again, by writing and by singing as often as I can *Me And A Gun*. It's like I refuse now to be a victim of my own guilt. I refuse to be a victim of not having a wonderful sexual experience again. And you are a victim when you can't allow yourself to have sexual pleasure again. I refuse to put all men in the same category, as I was doing. When something like that happens you do want to punish men, punish the ones that crushed the flower. But no one should choose to hold onto that hatred. It choked me. Sexually, I feel I won't be able to give completely and love to the extent, say, that I will want to have kids with him, for quite some time yet. I couldn't even consider that for a few years. I'm only beginning to fulfil myself now because I'm beginning to accept, and love, the parts of me, of woman, that I was trained to hate all my life. Particularly the bad girl I still can be."

Like Alanis Morissette, Tori Amos has translated her personal psychological traumas and revelations into a confessional performance which does not back down from the outrage many women feel, which has led music critics to place her in the school of "angry young women." "Give me peace, love, and a hard cock," she sings on *Professional Widow*, maintaining in her own explanation of the song that "you can't have one without the other." As she told Francesca Lia Block during an interview published in *Spin* in March 1996, "I really like her [the Professional Widow of the song] because she's dead honest. . . . People make statements about this unicorn shit and don't realize that 'this unicorn shit' was a secret code that millions of people were killed for. The gangs could learn a few things. . . . If you weren't toeing the Catholic line at the time, then you were a heretic. I'm trying to reconstruct some of these falsehoods. . . . One of the greatest lies that has been told, the lie about the sacred bride and the sacred bridegroom." Amos maintains that Jesus was the sacred bridegroom but the bride — or goddess — and her cults were wiped out by Christianity — making Mary Magdalene a whore instead of a priestess and taking away the Madonna's sexuality. "There's not a sacred bride in our culture. We kind of skulk off

Patti Smith Horses

KATE BUSH

THE WHOLE STORY

CRUCIFY
TORI AMOS

JONI
MITCHELL
TURBULENT
INDIGO

Joan Osborne
relish

S H E R Y L C R O W
Sheryl Crow
TUESDAY NIGHT
MUSIC CLUB
HOTEL
CALICO

Alanis
Morissette

into the darkness to fulfil these sides of ourselves. We get tied up or defecated on because we've judged our true desires as women so harshly. (If the bride had been acknowledged) there would have been honor of the feminine. There wouldn't have been patriarchy as we know it or matriarchy. There would have been balance. If you look at rock culture, there is very much a desire for the sacred bridegroom to die. The sacred brides don't die much. Janis Joplin is one of the very few."

Again, like Morissette, Amos is willing to relate her frustrations with the music industry itself. She told Albrecht Piltz, a writer for the German magazine *Keyboards*, in June 1992 that the music industry doesn't invest enough money in developing talent. "You know," she said, "if I wasn't doing what I'm doing now I'd gladly be on the other side, in Artist Development. I'd go out and listen to people, to find out who I could help — like what they used to do with people like Judy Garland. Because there are so many talents who have been playing only in clubs or in their living rooms, and people from the industry should care about them. They shouldn't wait until someone has the idea to look for a producer, somebody who knows how to make records and how to bring music from one medium, the piano or guitar in some living room or a club, to another, a tape or a record. I mean, you don't have to be a genius to know that the musicians are the backbone of the entire thing; without them there would be no music industry at all. . . . When you're afraid — afraid of being rejected — you can't express yourself in what you're doing. That awful album I made back then opened my eyes, that there are lots of people in the music business who either only reject you or fawn over you, that it's personally embarrassing to me. I've gotten to know both extremes, and both of them are just as damaging. They prevent you from finding yourself and create something that comes from here (lays her hand on her heart). Today I see it very clearly: What the music industry thinks is what it thinks, and what I think is what I think. When we're lucky we're thinking the same thing, but it's only important what I think. I needed a long time to come to this understanding."

While there may be a close connection between the work of Tori Amos and Alanis Morissette, music journalists have made much more of a perceived contrast between Morissette and musician /actor Courtney Love. There are indeed critics who gauge their questions about Morissette's alternative rock sincerity by utilizing Love as a counterpoint. Those who think of Morissette's transformation from dance artist to alternative voice as a shrewd public relations exercise endeavor to write Love into the scenario as a foil. Conversely, others who believe Morissette's evolution contains the integrity she maintains it does, present Love as their example of a successful public relations coup. Both Love and Morissette are making waves these days, though the former is doing so because of her appearance in the movie *The People Vs. Larry Flynt*. If there is any kind of debate going on between the principals themselves over who has integrity and who has not, they're being relatively quiet about it. Still, Holly Millea of *Premiere* magazine, in a profile of Love, does mention an MTV interview where Love has said Alanis Morissette's music is "a safe version of female rage" and then worries afterwards about whether the comment was "mean" or not. Her publicist, Pat Kingsley, assures her it was not.

The irony, of course, is that it is Love who is receiving the star treatment makeover to make her more palatable as a movie star, rather than the rock star who at one time presented a no-holds barred musical expression of *her* life experiences, which include working as a stripper, drug abuse, and the tragedy of husband Kurt Cobain's suicide. "Some of her best friends downplay the notion that this is a whole new Love," writes Millea. "'What kind of scrutiny is someone under that (if they) change their hair and lipstick color, they are instantly assumed to be a completely different person?' says R.E.M. singer Michael Stipe. 'She's really reaching the potential that I know she's always had.' But you don't hire a Pat Kingsley to tell you what shade of lipstick to wear. 'I called her at home in the middle of the night, crying,' Love says, 'and I said Pat, do you need a career challenge?'

'"She wasn't the first one to call me at four in the morning,' Kingsley recalls. 'I loved the idea that she wanted to change the perception about herself. We spent a lot of time talking about it.'"

But Love herself is aware that "the same establishment that

kept a wide professional berth from the car wreck of a singer can't get its arms around the Oscar-worthy actress fast enough."

"And what that is," Love told Millea, "is user-friendliness. I know a lot of it's fake. But I don't care! The welcome that I get from the grown-ups in the film industry is *so nice*. It frightens me. I'm used to going to a mall and having a kid with black lipstick scream at me, 'I love you! I didn't kill myself because of you!' Or, 'You suck!' But a grown-up in his 50s, in a suit, being nice? I melt. It's like being popular all of a sudden. You know? It's like losing a hundred pounds in public really quickly and not knowing you did — and not ever knowing you were fat."

Despite all the debate about integrity and who is more honest, who has had the makeover and who has not, there is no denying the impact of Courtney Love. "Love's confrontational stage presence with her band Hole, as well as her gut-wrenching vocals and power punk-pop songcraft, have made her a rock star in her own right," says *Rolling Stone*. And whether or not she is an antithesis of Morissette, her contribution to the new female voice of rock cannot be ignored.

Nor can British rocker Polly Jean Harvey, born in Yeovil, England in 1969. "Led by the talented guitarist, songwriter, and singer Polly Jean Harvey, the postpunk power trio PJ Harvey came from small-town England in 1991 and took London by storm with its raw, dynamic rock and Harvey's evocative / provocative female-centric lyrics," reports the *Rolling Stone Encyclopedia*. "In hypnotic tunes like *Dress, Happy and Bleeding* and *Sheela-Na-Gig,* Harvey sang about discovering, reviling, and revelling in her body. The tomboyish Harvey's discomfort with her femininity fueled her lyrics and image. *Dry*'s album cover features the androgynous artist skinny and bare-chested."

Harvey's next album, RID OF ME, contained lyrics which mocked efforts to "control her sexuality and art, taunting lovers on *Rid Of Me* and *Legs* and declaring her stature over cock-rockers on *50 Ft. Queenie*." Afterwards, a number of her fans were disappointed when Harvey denounced feminism in some interviews, though most admit her lyrics contradict the opinions she gives in her interviews. Harvey resists labels with a fierce passion, from being part of a female movement in rock music to even the label of genius which has dogged her for much of her career. She once told *Q* magazine in London that music has little to do with a performer's head. "It's to do with your body, which is a very sexual instrument."

Like Alanis Morissette, much is said about Sheryl Crow's transition from a pop back-up singer with the likes of Michael Jackson to the current artist on her own with her own music and her own direction. Like Morissette, there's an ongoing media investigation as to her legitimacy in what is, to some, a convenient change of direction. But as Crow succinctly puts it herself, "People can come and hear me play and determine whether I'm an artist or not."

Born in 1962 in Missouri, Crow found success with her first album after appearing at Woodstock '94. Influenced by her parents who were amateur musicians, she began to perform with rock groups when she was 16. Eventually she received a degree in classical piano from the University of Missouri and began to teach music at an elementary school in St. Louis. But in 1986, she moved to Los Angeles to pursue her own career, signing with A&M in 1991. From the very beginning she focused her songwriting on personal experiences relating to a woman including such subjects as sexual harassment. Her second album has moved into a broader range of social issues, however, as typified by her peers.

Since the success of her album TUESDAY NIGHT MUSIC CLUB, there's been a wide range of abuse heaped on her and she's not taking it lying down. As writer Elizabeth Renzetti pointed out in late 1996 in *The Globe and Mail*, "Sheryl Crow no longer reads what's written about her, because she's tired of reading 'stuff that would not even have come out of my mouth.' Does that mean writers completely fabricate material about her? Crow turns and projects disbelief with every ounce of her petite self. 'Are you *kidding*? I cannot count the number of times.' "

Like most women performers these days, she is at best amused about being incorporated into a female popularity slot trivialized as a trend and at worst annoyed about all the analysis of image change which she claims male stars rarely have to put up with. "Not to go off on the old man-woman thing, but it's definitely attached to being a female," she said. "John Lennon changed his image every five minutes but didn't get bogged down." It's the same old problem that Morissette has faced over image. And, like Morissette, Crow just keeps gritting her teeth and goes on with it. Her second album, SHERYL CROW, is as uncompromising as the bearing down she has had to manage over image. If you want to discuss backing up your principles of moral outrage, you'd best discuss it with Sheryl Crow who knows all about it.

"Then there's the matter of Wal-Mart, the huge discount chain that refused to stock her latest record . . . because of the lyrics in one song," wrote Renzetti. "In *Love Is A Good Thing,* she sings, "Watch our children while they kill each other / With a gun they bought at Wal-Mart discount stores." Wal-Mart, not appreciating this social commentary, gave Crow a choice. She could change the lyrics or sell her records elsewhere. She chose the latter and almost certainly has suffered for it."

Said Crow, "They have artists over a barrel, because (Wal-Mart) is one of the biggest places as far as record sales go . . . to change the lyrics would have meant I was lying so that I could get my record sold."

Her second album has been deemed dangerous, with "gun-toting teens, abortion-clinic shootings and spiritual emptiness" as themes, and was termed by Mark Jenkins in *The Washington Post* "a dark, feisty successor to her easygoing country-rock debut," an album with "a more aggressive sound and stance." As Crow explains, "People, particularly of my generation, are in deep need of something to believe in. A really good example of that is the fact people still flock to Graceland, and celebrate the anniversary of John Lennon's death."

Another artist often mentioned in the same breath as Morissette is Iceland's Bjork Gudmundsdottir. Born In Reykjavik in 1965, she grew up on rock music, usually of the sixties era. Recording her first album when she was only eleven, she ultimately joined the legendary hard rock band Theyr, evolved from that into a theatrical rock band called KUKL, which ultimately became the Sugarcubes. It wasn't until 1993 that Bjork came out with her first American solo album, DEBUT, which included a high-charting single *Human Behavior*. This album was followed in 1995 by POST.

Bjork possesses a powerful, "keening" voice but also a flair for lyrics which point to feminine self-possession and psychological balance, as seen in *Army Of Me*, lyrics which are reminiscent of Alanis Morissette's *Not The Doctor* or *Right Through Me*:

Stand up
You've got to manage
I won't sympathize
Anymore
And if you complain once more
You'll meet an army of me

— *Army Of Me*

And Bjork's song *Hyper-Ballad* seems to elucidate the contrasting fragility and assertiveness of today's modern woman:

We live on a mountain
Right at the top
There's a beautiful view
From the top of the mountain
Every morning I walk towards the edge
And throw little things off
Like
Car-parts, bottles and cutlery
Or whatever I find lying around
It's become a habit
A way
To start the day.

— *Hyper-Ballad*

Discussing her work on POST, Bjork admitted, in a conversation with Nathalie-Roze Fischer of *Muse* magazine, "It seems more aggressive and dark than DEBUT. The ideas that spin all the songs are independence, strength and instinct, but I think that there's a little more fear on this album. It's more honest and less naive about where I am in the present tense. POST explores happy stuff, but the dreams are mixed with reality."

And the concept of reporting and dealing with reality from the standpoint of independence is also presented by Kentucky songstress Joan Osborne, who was part of the Grammy nominating spree in 1996 when Morissette took home most of the awards. In her platinum selling debut album RELISH, she sings about a one-night stand, including a description of her "panties in a wad at the bottom of my purse," and on her hit single from the same album *One Of Us* wonders "What if God was . . . just a slob like one of us?" Perhaps not as profound in her questioning of traditional forms of faith as Tori Amos or Alanis Morissette, Osborne nevertheless gives depth to contemporary pop music.

Originally a student of film in New York, she evolved into music by performing gospel-flavored blues in various Manhattan nightclubs. Osborne is not only fascinated by blues but has avidly explored feminism, even volunteering in the past as an escort at a New York abortion clinic. According to *Rolling Stone* magazine, Osborne went so far as to wear a t-shirt bearing the emblem "Rock for Choice," the music community's largest pro-choice activist group, which she has supported for some time. In fact, the CD booklet for RELISH includes a suggestion that fans donate to Rock for Choice or any of three other feminist groups. And she includes the mailing addresses.

"Osborne's feminist studies have also influenced her spiritual views, which strongly color the lyrics on RELISH," wrote Ann Powers in *Rolling Stone*. "*One of Us* is 'a good song,' Osborne mutters, the way she might admit the niceness of a less-than-thrilling blind date. But she could talk for hours about the portrayal of Eve as the inventor of the kiss in *Lumina*, the sanctified street dealer of *St. Teresa*, the holy sex of *Dracula Moon* or the surreal fantasy about a sighted Ray Charles in *Spider Web*. There's a philosophy at work in Osborne's writing, one she's developed through years of reading authors like the religious theologian Elaine Pagels and the Greek mystical novelist Nikos Kazantzakis. It's a vision based on embracing a fall from grace."

Said Osborne, "I just don't necessarily see knowledge — being conscious and being an intellectual and a sexual creature — as a horrible state. Organized religion presents the garden of

Eden as this ideal of innocence and being sheep in the flock, unaware, as the goal. To me, that's just too passive; it's less interesting than the more dangerous and confusing but more satisfying state of actually being conscious — being able to come to God or spirituality with all of yourself, with your brain and your will and your curiosity and your sensuality and everything."

Today's crop of talented female artists are taking their musical art seriously but, more than that, see the impact of it on a world which is in search of new feelings and a sense of compassion. As Canadian singer/songwriter Sarah McLachlan told *Muse* magazine not long ago, there is sometimes a sense in an artist that they are people who can affect change in the world. "I think every day there's small moments of that," said McLachlan. "And I think everybody has that. You smile at a lonely old person and they smile back; you've given them something. You've made them smile, you know? That's as great a gift as raising a whole shitload of money for some charity. Sometimes I think just compassion for human beings is something that's really lacking in our day and age. I'd like to think that, yeah, I'm doing some good. Because I have this great opportunity. It's wild, some of the letters I get. People say I've really affected their lives and really helped them stir something. It's a really great feeling to know that. And also to know that I can stand up on stage and . . . this is where it gets frightening . . . I can be up on stage and I can sway people, one way or another, if I wanted to . . . . I have a big responsibility to use this gift properly. To do good things with and not do bad things. But, I mean, everbody's got that responsibility." McLachlan, who recorded her first album TOUCH, when she was only nineteen, hails from Nova Scotia. With albums such as SOLACE and FUMBLING TOWARD ECSTACY she has established herself in the vanguard of female artists who will likely have a tremendous impact on future audiences.

An even newer Canadian voice is Amanda Marshall whose self-titled debut album has done extremely well. Known for her powerful voice, she is also known for her outspoken remarks about artistic integrity, especially as it applies to the music machine. She has gone on record defending Alanis Morissette from critics who want to disparage her by introducing her dance record past in Canada. "So she made disco records when she was 16? Who cares? I mean so what? It's [*You Oughta Know*] a good song. Get up and dance. Shut up!"

As she told *Toronto Sun* writer Jane Stevenson, "All I can say is I made the record I wanted to make. People's antennae go up when they suspect that you are associated with as big a money-making machine as a company like Sony. I think they become suspicious and they start looking for things. But I don't think because you choose a more sort of commercial or legitimate, if you will, way of making records that makes you any less legitimate of an artist." And she was quick to point out that she appears on the album as her fully-clothed self.

These women are representative of many other artists, past, present and future, artists poised to bring a self-assertiveness and creative variation to rock music. They also are prepared to defend their ground against music pundits already dismissing them as a trend and questioning, as *USA Today*, put it, their "staying power." But staying power is not in the hand of the music pundits. It's not even in the hands of the record executives or, in some ways, the artists themselves. Rather, it is in the hands of the audiences. And who that audience is and what it feels for artists such as Alanis Morissette and her "army" indicates that there may be much more going on here than a brief infatuation with women performers or a trendy blip on the radar screen of music.

·eight·

Hand In My Pocket

Sometimes on stage I'm like a mirror. My music becomes less about me and more about what the audience sees in me that reminds them of themselves. I sense that some are there to release their own tension and frustration, and that's gratifying.

— *Alanis Morissette*

I feel drunk but I'm sober
I'm young and I'm underpaid
I'm tired but I'm working
I care but I'm restless
I'm wrong and I'm sorry baby
What it all comes down to
Is that everything's gonna be quite alright

— *Hand In My Pocket*

Although there may be a movement underway in contemporary rock and pop music to elevate artistic integrity beyond economic exigency, a view espoused by Alanis Morissette and many of her female peers, it has not apparently been founded on any contrived intention to do so by the artists or the music industry. Instead, this new movement has been made possible by the other side of the artistic equation, the overwhelming response of an audience eager to share in the feelings articulated by the performer. Not only must an artist have something to say to reach a large audience, but there must be a large audience out there anxious to listen. The fact that both prerequisites have been in place where Morissette is concerned is what has made the response to JAGGED LITTLE PILL so surprising, so uniformly worldwide, and so touchingly sanguine.

JAGGED LITTLE PILL was expected to do passably well all along. Initial response, after Morissette signed with Maverick, indicated that the album might go gold. In truth, that was all her management really required of it. Most careers are constructed gradually, and Morissette's, albeit a second incarnation for her musically, was expected to be no exception. Even most of those impressed with the work she and Ballard had done initially felt the same way about her album's prospects. As reported in the *Ottawa Citizen*, "Maverick picked up the record as it was, relatively unheard of in the music business, shipping it out last April (1995) without fanfare." Morissette's manager, Scott Welch, projected the album to be a solid success, selling over a 100,000 copies, but not a stunning success, and accordingly negotiated a higher than normal royalty rate for each album sold so as to ensure the cash advance would be recouped from sales. Even she did not seem to have great expectations for the work, nor did she seem to acknowledge the first signs of impending fame.

As reported in the *Ottawa Citizen*, Morissette's friend and voice teacher, Lynn Miles, arrived to stay with her in California in June 1995 only to discover that *You Oughta Know* was the most requested song in Los Angeles. But Miles reported that Morissette was "the same, sweet Alanis" who treated her life as she normally did, even in the face of fame, up early to handle her business on the telephone for about three hours, then off to the gym or to shoot the video for *You Oughta Know*. "She had an apartment in Santa Monica, a two-bedroom . . . nothing glamorous," said Miles. "She had, like, 300 candles melted all over the place and rooms full of (her) paintings, acrylics in abstracts."

"Just weeks before she began her reign atop the *Billboard* album charts, she busked unrecognized at a Santa Monica mall with Miles and her guitarist Ian Lefeuvre until a cop shooed them away," reported the *Citizen*. "They didn't earn a cent." Even when the first tour began, booked before the single of *You Oughta Know* and the album hit the charts, Morissette was not only self-effacing but nearly anonymous. Fans, not often recognizing her in the flesh, due in part to the way her appearance is deliberately veiled in the video for *You Oughta Know* and in part because she eschews a glamorous look, approached her outside concert venues, not looking for autographs, but wanting to ask for her ticket. As David Wild would later observe in his feature article an Morissette in *Rolling Stone*, "Here's a clue for the clueless generation: If you're going to worship someone, you ought to know what she looks like. Outside the Mercury Cafe Brewhouse, in Denver, where Alanis Morissette is playing a club gig, a desperate young man approaches the singer in the hopes of buying an extra ticket, unaware that he's talking to the headliner. It's a few hours before show time, and already a crowd of ticketless fans — a mix of intense young women, bookish lads and preppy couples — has gathered to buy scalped tickets to this sold-out show. Just because fans of Morissette connect with her heartfelt, earnest songs — in fact, they seem on the verge of anointing her rock's Generation X-rated diva — doesn't mean they could pick their heroine out of a police lineup."

Subsequent claims by the media that the album did so well from the very beginning of the release because of an immense Madonna-driven publicity campaign did not, in fact, reflect the truth. To the contrary, Morissette's management feared too much media exposure, especially since it was of more significance to them at the time to have Morissette tour with her new band so that they could obtain valuable performing experience together. Ultimately, she would play more than 250 concert dates worldwide over an 18 month period, initially touring small clubs, then gradually performing in larger and larger venues in several countries. But, at first, there was an urgency that she tour, even if it required her to play in small clubs and stay in less ostentatious hotels. She also passed on 1995 summer's Lollapalooza tour when she was asked to replace Sinead O'Connor. "A lot of people felt we were snubbing it," said manager Scott Welch. "I didn't feel she needed the pressure."

Nevertheless, influential music critic Timothy White of *Billboard* magazine had already written a rave review of the advance copy of JAGGED LITTLE PILL, and later observed that the success of the album "was a complete groundswell. It was from the public up, not the company down." Even Maverick's chief talent scout, Guy Oseary, claims to have intuited that the audience component would be there to acclaim Morissette's work, without any manipulation on the part of the label. "I sensed immediately that she was speaking to people and she'd be understood." Almost from the beginning, it appeared the audience had been waiting for someone like Morissette all along. When JAGGED LITTLE PILL's first single, *You Oughta Know*, was included on a compilation CD issued with a music magazine, an influential Los Angeles radio station decided to play the track. The actual single had not yet been issued to radio stations, but the airplay resulted in an immediate audience response. Said Welch, "We hadn't even started asking for it [airplay]. We hadn't even shipped the single yet. They started playing it. The phones lit up. And then when the phone lit up, bam, it went all over the country."

Most of Morissette's subsequent high profile publicity events — appearing on the MTV Awards and on the covers of *Spin* and *Rolling Stone* — were the result of requests from the parties concerned, not marketing efforts by management or Maverick. "I didn't twist anyone's arm to do that. They called and said, 'Would you do it?' We've really tried to limit our press exposure," said Welch.

On top of all this unexpected audience and media interest, the touring experience Morissette garnered also paid off very well. It resulted in a knock-out performance at the MTV Awards in New York. "This woman just got up there at Radio City Music Hall with no fear, in a house full of industry people, and blew their minds,'' said Welch. ''That audience was in shock. They were stunned when they finished. And like, Michael Jackson, TLC, Tom Petty, they were the first people up going 'wow!'. It was really a great night for her.'' And then there was a performance on *Saturday Night Live*. ''It's funny,'' said Welch, ''because she said to me, 'It's really scary, because growing up, if you were a musician you wanted to be in *Rolling Stone*, and you wanted to be on *Saturday Night Live*. Those things happened to me in the first six months.' ''

Notwithstanding the cynicism which greeted the transformation of Morissette from dance star to alternative rocker, a debate pro and con that took place among fans and detractors in the traditional media and on the Internet, where there are now over 8,000 web sites dedicated to Alanis, including the ''People Against Alanis Morissette Music'' or PAAMM page, the astounding initial success of JAGGED LITTLE PILL, which has continued unabated for more than a year and a half, demonstrates that from the very first moment the audience heard her work, they felt compelled to listen. Something in the soul-searching way in which she and Glen Ballard had written the material for the album had reached out to the same soul-searching character of an audience previously known for its hasty cynicism and even its deliberate hibernation within a condition of passive irony.

But what was and is that audience? What is the nature of that group of people known as Generation X or, these days, Generation XX? And what was it in the work of Alanis Morissette which caused them to swarm so persistently and completely around the songs and lyrics of JAGGED LITTLE PILL?

People, of course, are shaped a great deal by the tenor of their times; their times are usually shaped by developments, pressures, and even conspiracies which remain, for the most part, outside their control. This, arguably more than any other historical epoch, is one defined by loss of control, especially over individual ambition, in the face of so many developments and pressures outside our control. It is the age of loss of opportunity, of a shamefully narrow definition of human function and value. It is, in fact, an era of pervasive economic insecurity, of blatant manipulation at the hands of an unseen economic elite who have elected a free market as its god. Morissette's audience is a microcosm of the apparent victims of these various developments. "Apparent" victims because the struggle isn't over yet. If it was, JAGGED LITTLE PILL wouldn't have sold almost 20 million copies and Sheryl Crow would be making a deal with Wal-Mart rather than sticking to her principles.

And if it is true that we are a product of our times, it is equally true that each generation follows on the heels of its predecessor like the next boxcar in a long, continually chugging train. Each generation, in its time, reacts to its predecessor in the way incidents in a novel lead inexorably one to another. In this case, there would probably not be a Generation X if there had not been a so-called Sixties generation. And Generation X would not be the cynical generation it is without the idealism of the Sixties in the first instance and the incredible ease with which those ideals were abandoned in the second place. Generation X has a personality reflecting the rather ruthless forces which work increasingly upon it. It tends not to believe in very much because the last time it saw any ideals with which it could relate, in its fathers and mothers, those ideals evaporated in the vapid *kchink* of the cash register drawer.

Generation X has grown up within an atmosphere of ethical decay. As Generation X has reached its adulthood, it has had to deal with moral and political compromise on a massive scale, and it has come face to face with a society's decline. On the one hand, many human ideals evaporated because of an inherent foolishness perceived to be part of their very nature. As if idealism equals childish hope or charming but debilitating weakness. At the same time, whatever ideals have survived have been trivialized as secondary to the rise of business as the only true calling in human affairs, the only respectable vocation, the only understandable motivation in a material society which tends to measure all human value and function economically. A previous generation's demand for a clean environment has been essentially ignored. Its disgust with the cruelty of war has never translated itself into political will as the various wars continue unabated. The ideal that the individual is part of a society, with appropriate rights and responsibilities, has been undermined most of all by this move to break humans down into financial columns of profit and loss, revenue and cost. As the social rights were rationalized, the accompanying sense of responsibility to society decreased along with them. The sense that we are responsible for the enhancement of the human condition as a whole has been seriously compromised on the basis that the state of business maintains its cost is too high. Generation X, therefore, has resorted to desensitizing itself to the visible effects this abdication of human responsibility has displayed. Promised by their fathers and mothers that human standards of living would rise, members of Generation X have seen those standards decline instead, except for a small, new elite of morally decrepit privateers committed to the necessary sustaining of the required states of envy and contempt which will guarantee the profit they derive from such a society in decline.

The forces at play in western civilization at present are enough to make anyone cynical, are more than enough to drain the most stubborn beaker of its faith or hope. Over the past couple of decades, Generation X has suffered a gradual loss of citizenship in a "democracy" governed by business lobby rather than by the true wishes of the individual citizen or a workable concept of human empowerment. In the place of an enhanced society of free individuals, this generation has seen food banks, a diminishment of social safety nets, and an imposition of materialistic criteria as the only definition of human worth and function. It has been unemployed, underemployed, and, at best, exploitively employed. It has seen the educational function of its media vanish in favor of information conveyed in little packets of fluff designed for readers with the attention span of a hamster, while, at the same time, endorsing continued corporate initiatives designed to degrade the individual citizen to the advantage of the free market elite.

Generation X has invested in its education, then suffered the humiliation of not being able to use that education, waiting indefinitely on restaurant tables instead, wasting the credentials which would allow them to embark on much more. And the nature of that education itself has been manipulated to reinforce the notion that the only true worthwhile icon in society is the free market, the only vocation in which escape from mediocrity is possible is in business, and that exploration of the rights and responsibilities of the citizen is counter-productive where governments and business, working hand in hand, know what is best for everyone.

Generation X has found it impossible to believe in much because its governments have reduced expenditures in all areas which would have equalized opportunity and spurred initiatives for positive change. Instead, government has embraced a communications technology with much potential for human betterment and reduced it to a magnetic strip of unemployment, consumer acquiescence, disenfranchisement, and material gain. Unemployed, insecure in employment, cynically aware that what were once practical ambitions have now been reduced to unlikely fantasies, Generation X has been left with one unpalatable option: join the business march into the next millennium and continually worsen the gap quaintly called "economic change," or live forever on the fringes of society like some kind of collective alley cat. Wear the designer labels or dress yourself in rags. It's not much of a choice. And still fresh in this generation's mind is the preceding generation's promise that none of these things would happen and that same preceding generation's failure to live up to its ideals. It's a generation which has been forced to absorb a wide range of betrayal.

Still, it isn't political or economic issues which strike chords directly for audiences in the lyrics of Alanis Morissette or her peers. It's the personal side of the equation, the personal impact of all that has failed in recent years which Generation X feels the most and which is contained in the words expressed by their pop culture leaders. Regardless of what has been done for political or economic reasons in our society, most members of this society feel it in a more personal, apolitical way. They feel it in family breakdown, in the loneliness of children who do not understand why their parents are working all the time or why the relentless pressure to succeed or even survive economically too often ends up in marriage breakdown. They feel it in their desensitization towards violence, in high suicide rates. They feel it every time a philosophical ideal is translated into political correctness, shaming it as an ideal, the ensuing confusion over what is right because it is human and what is right because it is socially required. And they feel it every time the reality of their difficulty, whatever it may be, is swept under the carpet with manipulation of language. To rename as economically challenged someone who is poor doesn't change the suffering. They're *still* poor.

Generation X is the generation asked to stand in the corner where there really is no floor. The floor — personal security, economic security, faith in an ideal, political honesty, the right to dream, the right to individual self-empowerment, a sense of being a citizen in a society with rights and responsibilities, the right to family, the right to love, the right to some truth for a change, the right to respect, the right to a healthy environment — has been pulled out from under them by forces outside most people's apparent control.

And so, in the arena of rock music, which has been so often a mirror of society and its ever-growing ailments, there has been an explosion of rage. But the rage is becoming outrage and the outrage may become empowerment. As Sheryl Crow has stated, people are rather desperate for something to believe in. And as Alanis Morissette has said, when she performs she feels the audience reaching out to find something valuable in what she has learned about integrity, self-empowerment, the right to be outraged, and, inevitably, the ability to rise above your own cynicism to believe in what can be changed.

Her audience and the audience of her "army" of peers is Generation X. And Generation X is the collective victim of all that has been allowed to fail in the past 25 years, the group which, until now, has maintained that a state of belief itself may be beyond their ability to believe. But no matter how fierce your refusal to believe, you cannot help but believe in yourself, in your own self-empowerment, and, finally, in how that self-empowerment can often reach out to enhance eventually the human condition. Perhaps that is what is happening here and now as women lead the legions into a state of emotional honesty.

And in the concert hall, when Alanis Morissette stalks the entirety of the stage, one hand a fist, her voice crying her outrage into a microphone, the other hand in her pocket, a giant, hopeful audience pantomimes her gestures and sings along with her words from *Hand In My Pocket*:

I'm broke but I'm happy
I'm poor but I'm kind
I'm short but I'm healthy, yeah
I'm high but I'm grounded
I'm sane but I'm overwhelmed
I'm lost but I'm hopeful baby
What it all boils down to
Is that everything's gonna be fine fine fine
I've got one hand in my pocket
And the other one is giving a high five
—*Hand In My Pocket*

"People told me I should listen to her, but I refused for months because of her past history — a little Canadian pop queen who decided to go cool. I was sure it would suck. Then I heard a song on the radio and said, 'Hey, this is good. Who is it? She has a strong voice and her lyrics can touch anyone who has ever had problems in a relationship. Not only with a boyfriend, but with family or a friend, whatever. She made a complete about-face and gained respect. That's hard to do."

The speaker is Elaine Ostopkevich, 24, who, according to writer Jane Joyce in an August 1996 story in the *Montreal Gazette*, "came to love Morissette grudgingly and by accident."

Joyce is likewise tuned to this apparently puzzling aspect of Alanis Morissette, where she wins admiration even from the most begrudging. "In some circles, people love to slag Alanis Morissette ('She cashed in, she sold out, she's from Ottawa . . .')," she writes. "But if nobody likes her, how has she sold 14 million copies of JAGGED LITTLE PILL?" She went on to answer her own question. "The majority of Morissette's fans are female, and the ones I talked to had one reason in common for being fans; they love her lyrics. They can relate. She tells it like it is in a simple, raw manner. She doesn't sugar-coat nor does she victimize herself. And because she stays down-to-earth in the face of worldwide fame without dressing herself up and cashing in on the babe thing like so many women in rock, they don't find her intimidating. She's just like them. Women finally have an ally, and girls someone to look up to — someone who is clearly a strong person and who loves herself, yet acknowledges her emotional vulnerability without whining. There are worse role models."

And there are fans, whether male or female, who have the sense that the Alanis Morissette of JAGGED LITTLE PILL is not far removed from the Alanis Morissette who recorded her two earlier albums in Canada. "Dwight, 22, has been a fan since Morissette's early days, something hardly anyone dares to admit. He owns her dance albums ALANIS and NOW IS THE TIME along with JAGGED LITTLE PILL.

"She comes across as being intelligent," said Dwight. "At first I didn't like JAGGED LITTLE PILL. It was a total turnaround that took some getting used to, but it was a refreshing new sound. It's well put together lyrically and I love her raw voice. She's in your face and she speaks her mind. I knew she was a talent from the beginning and that she wouldn't just be a flash in the pan. She's an incredible performer and she's proud of being Canadian, which is nice for a change." ("This is the last show on our Canadian tour," Morissette said in Barrie a week later. "We've had an amazing time. Canadians are the best people in the world. It's our cross to bear.")

The interesting aspect about Morissette's continued relationship with her audience is that critics and writers who review her shows, while acknowledging the crowd's view of her, cling to the notion that it is either an extraordinary inexplicable stroke of fate or, as always, canny marketing. "There's a strangeness about this level of success," wrote Norman Provencher of the *Ottawa Citizen* in August 1996. "There's a spookiness any time someone captures the emotions and desires of millions of people, whether it's in politics or rock music. Why does it happen to someone like Morissette and not, say, to someone equally (some would say more) deserving like Liz Phair or PJ Harvey? A lot has been made of the revenge component in Morissette's material, spurred by her first single *You Oughta Know*, every cad's middle-of-the-night phone call from hell. Too quickly, it seems people picked up the theme: 'Angry young woman comes back to settle accounts.' And there is a lot of that to Morissette's stuff, but there's no way you're going to sell 14 million records on one thought. As her record label marketers are making clear, there's more to Morissette than nails in the eyes. The more you listen to JAGGED LITTLE PILL, the more it becomes apparent there are many more emotions at play. Maverick Records' marketing department has shrewdly set about releasing singles that capitalize on the range of thoughts and musical forms on the record. Truth be told, the range isn't *that* broad. We're not dealing with Dylan (either Thomas or Zimmerman) or Joni Mitchell here. Each song features a main idea surrounded by what sound like high school diary entries, often saved from banality by a quirky vocal or catchy musical bridge from producer Glen Ballard. But the point is, the songs connect because most kids have a diary, if only in their heads. Youth is the time of the first big emotions and any artist who pinpoints the pain and wonder will be a millionaire sooner or later."

But Morissette has said it herself. "I wish I had had me to listen to when I was fourteen."

"To many of her fans, Alanis Morissette is more than a homegrown rock star with a slippery voice and an album of catchy songs. Judging by conversations with members of the predominantly female crowd that flocked to the Corel Centre on Friday to see her show, she's seen as a tough role model who's not afraid to express herself. The fact that she's Canadian — and from Ottawa — is a bonus," wrote Lynn Saxberg in the *Ottawa Citizen* just two days after Provencher's piece appeared in print. Among the comments Saxberg accumulated from teens attending the concert were: "I like her because she writes from her heart, she expresses her feelings." And, "I like her voice, her style. Her songs can relate to things in real life." And, "She's way over the top. She has guts."

The same themes keep coming up. Guts, honesty, moving lyrics, comments demonstrating that Morissette has become a kind of voice for belief, if not in an alternative direction for society, at least in being in touch with self, and the pain and anger this era has generated in the young. "Sometimes on stage I'm like a mirror," Morissette told *Q* magazine in 1996. "My music becomes less about me and more about what the audience see in me that reminds them of themselves. I sense that some are there to release their own tension and frustration, and that's gratifying."

The political and economic issues may not be mentioned but the plight of Generation X is in the wings of the concert stage just the same. It's the loneliness and the frustration of it all, the disenfranchisement, the sense of betrayal, then, evolving from that, the anger, the outrage, the "guts" and the forthrightness of the overall complaint, evolving of course into songs of hope and anthems of shared faith. "I see the whole concept of Generation X implies that everyone has lost hope," Morissette told writer Mark Brown in the *Edmonton Journal*. "I can agree with that, and I can understand why; things like my parents coming out of high school or university with five or six jobs waiting for them, and people my age coming out of university with a degree and every reason to get jobs and having no potential jobs and being in the same position as someone who left high school in grade 8. Just our times are different. So obviously, our mind-sets are going to be different. But at the same time I don't think that an entire generation should be underestimated. I happen to be lucky in that I knew what I wanted to do as far as a career since I was nine years old. I was blessed in that I could tap into what I loved to do that turned me into something that could put food on my table at a very young age. That's the only difference I see between myself and anyone else my age."

The pressure to succeed and the pressure to fit into a social mold of acceptable behavior. Morissette has always been candid about the influence of these concepts on her life. "It started from a very young age," she told John Pareles in the *New York Times*. "I just wanted to be what society and your environment and this world leads you to believe, that if you're externally successful and you're smart and you have high grades and you have a lot of money that you're a good person. And if you don't have those things, and if you're not esthetically living up to what the standard is either, then you're not a good person. That's ludicrous to me now, but I gave in to it fully when I was younger."

Wrote Pareles, "At her sold-out show at Roseland, Ms.

Morissette uses every inch of space. She bounds from one end of the broad stage to the other, wearing a lose white shirt that grows ever more disheveled; her long hair hangs over a sweaty veil that she keeps flipping back over her shoulder. Her voice can be gentle or cutting, but in the songs from JAGGED LITTLE PILL, it is never alone. The voices of hundreds of teenage girls are raised along with hers, sharing every word — a choir trading low self-esteem for solidarity."

Writer Lynn Margolis of the *Pittsburgh Tribune* also noted, in a review of a Morissette concert at St. Vincent College there, the startling relationship she has with her audience. "Though they seemed relatively sedate," she wrote, "they sang along as a leather-slacked Morissette performed every one of the 13 songs from her multi-platinum album, JAGGED LITTLE PILL. They screamed every time she addressed them, raised fists every time she delivered a particularly relevant lyric in a repertoire of profane kiss-off, poignant longing and acute observations. They also listened raptly as she exercised her pretty soprano on such songs as *Wake Up, Not The Doctor*, and *Head Over Feet*, backed by her tight four-piece band. And they put up with the bizarre vocal exercises she sometimes performed, stretching her strong, often nasal voice any way she could.

"From the opening harmonica notes of *All I Really Want* it was clear that the reason Morissette has hit so big is because she has a message that resonates — not just among women — and a delivery that's nothing if not well-polished. Though she's got tons of cheerleaders among females who are thrilled someone is finally saying what they've thought for so long, she's also got legions of guys who love the idea of a chick singing about sex in a theater, about sex at all. Yet she doesn't stand onstage and flaunt sexuality; she doesn't need to — she sings about it instead. . . . That she cannot be seen as an act that appeals to women only — or who plays to male fantasies — is part of what makes her so interesting," said Margolis.

Morissette admits that the audience changes from time to time, in shape and nature, even while she knows the common bond between her and the crowd is that sense of empowerment both her and her fans appear to derive from frank admission of their feelings, outrage and vulnerability. She has stated that she will not resist any emotion that finds its way into music. "If it writes itself into a song," she told Los Angeles writer Fred Shuster, "I don't question it. I'm empowered by my vulnerability and not apologetic at all for it." As for the audience. "I see everybody, every shape and form. Some nights it will be predominantly young women. In Amsterdam, I was surprised to see something like 98 percent males."

Toronto Star writer Peter Howell had an opportunity to explore the male component of the fascination for Morissette prior to a performance in New York City in February 1996. "Ralph Dano and Marco Matteo are men on serious missions for Alanis Morissette, the reigning queen of new rock," he wrote. "Dana, 19, from Brooklyn, is planning to ask the Ottawa-born Morissette, 21, to marry him. Matteo, 25, from Washington, N.J., has humbler ambitions. He just wants to give Morissette his found art collection of photos, a woodpecker feather and an Indian cutting stone. The two are inside the Roseland Ballroom, once the home of elegant waltzing and foxtrotters, today a cavernous rock club. They're awaiting the first of Morissette's three sold-out concerts here, and discussing how best to approach the object of their intense affections."

"I was just going to say to her, 'I know you're not going to say yes, but I just have to ask you,'" Dana said about his proposal of marriage. He also appeared to appreciate that Morissette's message is more than some give her credit for. "It's that whole female *angst* thing, but that's just on the surface. Once you get into her album and read her lyrics, it's incredible." Matteo on the other hand had a more spiritual mission. "I saw her when they were dropping her off for soundcheck. I just wanted to run up to her, but I didn't. I have an 8 X 10 frame of pictures I want to give her. They show a row of corn and a sunset, with a nasty storm approaching. I know she's very spiritual and stuff. I've also got a feather off a woodpecker that I found on the ground. I stuck it on the glass inside. . . ." He also possessed a chipped red stone. "It's a Jasper stone, which the Indians used to use for cutting. New Jersey used to be Indian territory. I just want her to have it."

Assorted female fans have more typical opinions. "She's got a powerful voice. I can relate to her music." Or "She's around our age and she *knows*." And "She sticks up for women. She's honest. She tells the truth."

There's a refreshing charm in the candid simplicity of what the audience is saying. It doesn't sound like cynicism and it doesn't sound like it's trapped inside the state of irony which more noticeably seems to emanate from music critics, psychologists, and the unrelenting voices of Morissette's backlash detractors. Said New York rock critic Ira Robbins, "I think she's just a strong, aggressive character, and in the '90s, people really mistake aggression for strength."

"Alanis Morissette is an angry woman to some, but experts and fans say the emotion is reality," wrote Shelly Decker for the Sun Media Corporation in August 1996. "Performing a sold-out Coliseum show Saturday, the Ottawa-born singer has shocked some with her get-tough, don't-take-any-crap attitude. Among her critics she's viewed as an opportunist exploiting Gen-X angst. But to her fans she is a fresh breath of real life against a tired train of love songs and sobbing broken hearts." Decker gives the psychologists their say, reporting that "musicians, like other artists, often express emotions in their work. It can be a healthy way of working through the emotion." Psychologists report that "women tend to be co-operative, helpful and tackle issues quietly, but they can also get mad" and "often the emotion is sparked among women because they feel they don't have a voice." In addition, women may feel they don't get support at home, have to face sexual harassment at work, infidelity, equal pay for equal work issues, financial problems, and abusive relationships.

Ironically, some who examine Morissette's profound affect on her audience do not take into serious consideration what the audience is saying and the generation of frustrated people her audience represents. The true irony emerges, for example, in a long *Washington Post* article written by Richard Leiby in April 1996, focusing on what, indeed, is true irony, as it relates to Morissette's song *Ironic*. According to Leiby's rather lengthy tome, after interviews with various English professors and assorted experts, he deems Morissette's *Ironic* as not that ironic at all. "Isn't it ironic? Sorry, Alanis, but no, it isn't. The gazillion-selling singer is back on top of the charts with a song and video about a series of events that qualify as annoying or unfortunate, but wouldn't pass for ironic in most freshman English courses," wrote Leiby. What follows is more than 1,300 words about what is truly ironic, the various kinds of irony, expert consultation, and finally application of the entire mess to Morissette's song. One of the academic views comes from Paul Fussell, Professor Emeritus of English at the University of Pennsylvania and author of *Bad: Or, the Dumbing of America.* "Like most older academics, Fussell has never heard Morissette's song," Leiby reports. "Surprisingly (but not ironically), he praised her lyrics after they were read to him. 'Those are some pretty nice words,' he says. 'It's good for what it is. It's sardonic, and very little pop culture is.' Some of the lyrics pass Fussell's test for "situational" irony, but he flunks them for "rhetorical" irony. 'Rhetorical irony requires immense intellectual self-respect," Fussell instructs. "You have to be more or less brilliant to get rhetorical irony.'" Etc.

In the end, what's troubling about all this intellectual bafflegab instead is that all the causes of Generation X anger and frustration end up reduced to a dictionary definition of what irony actually is, and then the world continues on as it always did. The other irony is that the audience is meshing so powerfully behind singers like Morissette because they can relate to them, but in the world outside of their control, no one is really listening. They're simply debating the accuracy of a word.

Or else the debate about Morissette's staying power goes on, again apparently diffusing the audience response and the nature of the audience responding. *USA Today*'s analysis of various women artists before the 1996 Grammy Awards program gave Mariah Carey the nod, generally speaking, as the artist with staying power. Yet one pundit contacted for his opinion, music consultant Jeff Pollack, recognized that artists such as Alanis Morissette and Joan Osborne have struck a chord with audiences who do not wish to be manipulated by trend. "Alanis and Joan have deep records with real substance. Rather than being overhyped, they were embraced by a grass-roots audience, the best route to success. That's good news for all of us who welcome new music," he told writer Edna Gundersen.

For her part, Morissette is still presenting the honesty which her audience says it admires. As she explained it to Julene Snyder in *Bam* in July 1995, "I think a lot of the reasons there's been a lot of internal success for me — I'm not talking about external success right now — the reason I've arrived at the place I'm at right now personally and spiritually is because I made so many mistakes. And I don't regret any of them. The main advice I'd give to young musicians is 'don't be afraid to fuck up.' I sure did."

But the internal success is linked to the external success. It's the internal success which is drawing the audiences. And this "grass-roots" attraction is taking place regardless of a status quo analysis of the attraction which does not quite own up to the social, political, economic, and ethical compromises a greedy society has made, and the resulting vacuum which has been created in the hopes and dreams of most of an entire generation.

Ironically, this caution(above) against listening to JAGGED LITTLE PILL *posted at the People Against Alanis Morissette Music (PAAMM) site on the World Wide Web provoked her web-fans to block entry into the PAAMM site. Others in the media have paid ironic tribute with caricatures (below).*

·nine·

Can't Not

I was auditioning not only their musicianship, but also if they understood what I was singing in my songs. I mean, I never came out and posed the question, "Do you understand where I'm coming from?" But I did get a sense from them whether they did. It's a very precious thing to me, the creation of art, and the process I go through to create is something I hold really dear.

— *Alanis Morissette*

I'd be lying if I said I was completely unscathed
Would I be putting it right with my silencer, rage
Would I be letting you in, inviting a reaction, yeah
And how would I explain ...
Because I can't not
Because I can't not
Because I can't not win without losing, my dear

— *Can't Not*

Alanis Morissette's commitment to her audience is clear in the care and energy she puts into her live performances, including the selection of her band. The first tour after the release of JAGGED LITTLE PILL was arranged by management in order for Morissette to gain some valuable experience performing live with her new band. After auditioning several musicians, she settled on guitarist Jesse Tobias, formerly of the band Mother Tongue and recommended by the Red Hot Chili Peppers' Flea and Dave Navarro, who performed with her on the album version of *You Oughta Know*, drummer Taylor Hawkins, bassist Chris Chaney, and former King Swamp guitarist Nick Lashley. Morissette told *Spin* that the band just worked out for her. "If I wasn't in a band with them I would probably have dated each one of them already, except Nick, who's married. But it's too sacred for us to jeopardize our professional relationship."

Tobias, ironically enough, enjoyed a short stint with one of rock music's most macho acts, Red Hot Chili Peppers, before joining Morissette, "one of pop's leading exponents of Nineties feminine sensibilities." Tobias was a member of that group for only two months before he was replaced by Dave Navarro. He also arrived in Los Angeles around the same time as Morissette, and as a result they had stories to trade about the music scene in general. "We talk about that sometimes. She dealt with a lot of the same people I did, in both good and bad ways. And we talk about all the weasels and the scenesters, and how we survived all that with our dignity intact. It was an exciting time in my life, living on Sunset and Fuller with a band and trying to get signed," he said.

Tobias was the first guitar player to try out for Morissette and Taylor Hawkins was the first drummer. "I'm a very rhythmic player and Taylor and I locked in together automatically. I think it was two days later that they called us and offered us the gig," Tobias explains. Nick Lashley had already played with Chrissie Hynde and Canadian singer Sass Jordan, while Chris Chaney did time with pop star Christopher Cross in the 1980s.

While selecting her band, Morissette sang three songs with three different people every half-hour for two days straight, she has reported. "Those guys stood out. I was auditioning not only their musicianship, but also if they understood what I was singing in my songs. I mean, I never came out and posed the question, 'Do you understand where I'm coming from?' But I did get a sense from them as to whether they did. It's a very precious thing to me, the creation of art, and the process I go through to create is something I hold really dear. So I wanted to get a sense that they were excited by it, too."

Morissette attempts to have her live performance contain the same potential for spontaneity that her creation of JAGGED LITTLE PILL did in Glen Ballard's studio. "The whole idea behind JAGGED LITTLE PILL was that it was created spontaneously in the studio. There's something to be said for just letting a song become what it wants to be in a live show."

Before the new line-up went on tour, there was a performance set up for Maverick executives. As Morissette told *Mojo*, "It started with a kind of pseudo-gig. . . . So we asked some Maverick people down. We ended up with 300 instead of eight. Madonna came. No pressure, it was only Madonna."

As the band began to tour, Morissette became increasingly convinced they were the right musicians to play with her. Not only was she enlisting their help in continuing to master the guitar herself, but she wanted musicians who, though experienced, still enjoyed the world of performing rock music. As Alan di Perna reported in *Guitar World Online* in September 1996, "Alanis Morissette walks the line between total self-possession and complete self-abandonment. She gives it up 100 percent for the audience but, to all appearances, she doesn't lose her cool amid the mass adulation, media sniping and rigors of the road. She expects the same of her band. The four players are well chosen. To a man, they're seasoned enough to handle the gig, but not so experienced that they've become jaded."

Said Morissette, "None of us are. That was quite important to me in choosing these musicians. I didn't want to work with people who had done it for decades and were just really tired of the touring process. I needed to feel that they had passion. Because I didn't want to deny myself the pleasure of my own greenness, and the wide-eyed 'in-aweness' that I had. I didn't want to have to suppress that excitement because I was surrounded by people who were sick of the whole thing. But they've all turned out to be just amazing in this band." And the band members feel the same way about Morissette. "She's refreshingly nice to work with," said Nick Lashley. "She encourages us to put our own personalities and our own creativity into the music, which isn't always the case when you go on the road as a hired-gun guitarist."

Since beginning touring, Morissette has begun playing more guitar, both electric and acoustic. Lashley and Tobias claim she is an incredibly quick learner. "About two years ago, I realized there was nothing to stop me from learning guitar," she said. "So I picked one up and started playing. In the past, the guitar had always intimidated me. I don't know why, really. I started playing piano when I was six, and piano can be equally intimidating. But guitar is something different. I've been playing a lot of electric lately. I'm fascinated by an instrument that can express, sonically and musically, the same emotions that I'm feeling."

For di Perna, "What comes across most about Morissette, even more than her sturdy intelligence, is her incredible self-possession. The woman seated cross-legged and calm in her dressing room seems an entirely different person from the one who was just on stage a few seconds ago, flailing away at a white Stratocaster during soundcheck, working harder than some artists do during their shows. And that's nothing compared to what will happen in a few hours, before a crowd of several thousand young girls in roughly the same state of hysteria as those fanatical Christians who have themselves nailed to crosses at Easter. For the faithful gathered inside the Greek Theater this evening, all attention, all devotion, is focused on the figure on stage in the loose white blouse and black leather pants, hair whipping around like tassels on a Tibetan prayer wheel."

When writer Karen Bliss caught up to Morissette and her band just before the 1996 Juno Awards, for an article in *Canadian Musician*, they had become a seasoned and tightly-knit group, due to their respect for Morissette, her refusal to bestow any star treatment on herself, and her ability to communicate. "Alanis Morissette is not queen of intimidation. She's queen of communication," said Bliss. "Whether it's through her honest lyrics or honest conversation, she has this ability to bring you into her space. The music on JAGGED LITTLE PILL is all about opening up, exposing the wounds then allowing them to heal. That's why she has sold millions upon millions of albums. People appreciate and identify with her. She's speaking the minds of millions. Her ability to communicate continues onstage. That's where the spellbinding singer immerses herself in her words and throws her entire body into the songs. And that's where her band . . . supports and surrounds her, and helps her take the songs to a higher degree of intensity and meaning."

Bliss went on to say, "Whereas her first appearance in Toronto at the Velvet Underground and, to a lesser degree, at Lee's Palace, was a bit disjointed — Morissette doing her vocal acrobatics as the band played along — with the latest RPM Warehouse gig, there was energy that connected the performance and a freedom to explore within the songs. Igniting and spontaneous, this was not a bunch of hired guns. It was a full round of ammunition." Suggesting Morissette and the group have become soulmates, Bliss notes that despite Morissette's success they continue to hang out together. They travel on the same bus and are booked into the same hotels. And the band has an unusual amount of respect for her.

"The first gig we ever did with her in Banff, she took control," said Lashley. "She had a vibe that she was going to be a very strong performer right from the get-go." The band turns its monitors up to stay in tune with Morissette's performance and, if there is a sour note which gets played, everyone ignores it in favor of keeping the electricity of the performance going. "After a gig, we go straight to our dressing room, all of us, and sit around and talk the shit out of each other for half-an-hour. It's positive. And that's the main thing, the music. That's the main thing for her too. I mean, that's what it's about," Lashley observed.

In addition, Morissette is reportedly encouraging about not only having the bandmembers get involved with the songwriting and material for the next album but in making adjustments to the live versions of material from JAGGED LITTLE PILL. "It just came through jamming around through rehearsals, and through accidentally falling upon things," said Lashley. "She actually encouraged us to not stick rigidly to the album. We've written songs in soundcheck with her and we wrote a song in a hotel room in Buffalo. We've seen the way she works. She's genuinely, amazingly talented. The way she can improvise a melody over a piece of music. I've never seen anything like it. The reason this album is doing so well is because they're brilliant songs."

While the marriage between Morissette and her band appears to be made in heaven, and while audiences continue to respond to both JAGGED LITTLE PILL and the excitement of her live performances, as the band continued its gruelling world tour, reviewers began to climb on board as well, for the most part raving about the force and directness of her material and its presentation. As Nicolas Jennings wrote in *Maclean's*, "Honesty, in fact, is the quality reviewers cite most in praising the new songs. Timothy White, editor of the influential music-industry weekly *Billboard*, described JAGGED LITTLE PILL as 'spellbindingly frank,' adding that 'her wounded outrage mingles with a gathering courage that gives the listener a giddy desire to cheer her on.'"

Citing her resistance to aloofness which so-called angry singers take as their trademark and a sometimes trendy antagonism towards their audiences, the *Boston Globe* concentrated on her release and the healing theme in her music. "Morissette succeeded on Saturday despite having several things stacked against her. First, she had a terrible cold, she confessed when she stepped off her bus drinking a cup of tea on her way to the dressing room. Second, she was frazzled because she had an all-night ride to New York ahead of her, then a 4:30 a.m. video shoot in Manhattan for the song *You Learn*. And third, she was playing in the sonic hellhole that is the Gosman Center — the gym sounds okay when the Celtics use it for rookie camp in the summer, but it is an acoustic abomination for concerts. Morissette's show was only 65 minutes long because she deleted a few songs to protect her voice. . . . Otherwise she stuck to the JAGGED LITTLE PILL album, breathing new air into the arrangements and, amid a dramatic light show of strobes and other effects, leaving the impression of an immense talent who will stick around for years to come."

"Morissette's young," wrote concert reviewer Greg Forman from Charleston, South Carolina. "Merely by proving she's an artist, rather than some producer's pet project, allows her live performances to establish credibility. Her ability to make her audience passionately identify with emotional turmoil is one of the better byproducts of alternative's massive success — even as her popularity (and her lack of conflict with popularity) pushes her beyond alternative's boundaries. If she can manage to make her music and images seem an organic part of her emotional life, she could develop into one of rock's best artists."

And, as if to point out the connection between the spontaneity which resides in the live presentation of music and the more pre-planned art of recorded music, Jeff Giles of *Newsweek* wrote in August 1995, "Craftmanship can be a hell of a bore, and Morissette's at her best when the melodies, like the lyrics, seem to float off the top of her head, as in fabulously carefree and shuffling tunes like *Hand In My Pocket* and *You Learn*. In this day and age, PILL may not be a shocker, but it's the next best thing: a pleasant surprise."

If there is honesty in having songs "float off the top of her head," concert reviewers have noted how audiences respond to her honesty during her live performances. Marisa Fox recounts this exchange between Morissette and her audience: "'Why are you so mad?' Alanis Morissette asked mockingly of the crowd at Roseland Tuesday night, before whipping her long brown hair back and forth, pummeling the air with her fists and launching into *You Oughta Know*, her signature song of a scorned lover's wrath. With that, Morissette — Canada's one-time answer to Debbie Gibson turned into modern-day Medusa for Madonna's Maverick label — insured the crowd would be hers. She dismissed skeptics who doubt the authenticity of her music, her image as Miss Female Rage '96 and her Grammy-nominated, multi-platinum album, JAGGED LITTLE PILL. And she let her fans know that she — like them — is no mere rebel without a cause."

Nor have the raves emanated purely from North America. "Alanis Morissette, who appeared in concert at the SFX in Dublin last night, is the latest in a growing line of successful women in rock," wrote Kevin Courtney for *The Irish Times* in April 1996. "And her quirky, mannered vocal style, combined with her edgy, brutally honest tunes, have struck a raw nerve in pop's collective psyche. Her third album, JAGGED LITTLE PILL, is top of the charts in the U.S., and songs like *Hand In My Pocket, You Oughta Know* and *You Learn* have set the airwaves alight with their adult subject matter and measured, mature observations. . . . After her second album, however, the young Morissette moved to Los Angeles and the transformation to intense, intelligent woman's icon began. She signed to Madonna's Maverick label, which on the face of it might seem the perfect outlet for Morissette's sexually candid lyrics. Alanis is no exhibitionist, however, and while Madonna might revel in the accoutrements of pain and pleasure, Morissette is more concerned with the hurt and heartache beneath the shiny sexual surface. . . . Last night's concert at the SFX sold out in one day, but Morissette returns to Dublin on July 14th to play the Point Depot, where she will distribute even more of those jagged, cathartic little pills to an eager, empathic audience."

And the Canadian Press news service reported a glowing review from Australia only a few weeks later, noting the remarks by reviewer Ian MacFarlane of *The Australian* after she played Brisbane's Festival Hall. "Morissette is a challenging performer," MacFarlane wrote. "Any expectations go straight out the window. Where she has it over the likes of Salt 'n' Pepa, Janet Jackson, TLC and even Madonna, for that matter, is that her music and lyrics have genuine depth. Her music is neither sweetness and light nor dance-oriented. As played by her band on Saturday night, she music was at times crashing rock, and at other times delicate and refined."

According to MacFarlane, "There are no half-measures with such a performer. It's all or nothing, and the audience responded with appropriate vigor. In fact, I'd be hard-pressed to recall louder screams of approval for such a spirited performance. I many not know the words to her songs, but I know a good performance when I see one. Morissette is an artist imbued with a rare degree of skill and all-encompassing passion."

As Morissette performed across Canada on her "Can't Not" tour about a year after the release of JAGGED LITTLE PILL, some reviewers were grudgingly beginning to admit that perhaps the quality of her live performance testified to the honesty in the music after all. "The last time Alanis Morissette was here in Calgary, she was signing autographs at Southcentre," wrote Tyler McLeod for the *Calgary Sun*. "Morissette triumphantly returned a superstar. Last night proved to be a test of whether Alanis is performer or product. Even away from her studio and producer Glen Ballard, she passed the test with flying colors. When her hand wasn't too busy making a peace sign, she had the crowd wrapped around her finger. Her sound had a decidedly harder edge than her album, though it did not detract from her appeal. The one constant in Alanis' career from pop queen to riot grrrl has been an unfailing knack for melody. She's able to toss out a number that instantly becomes committed to memory. This fact was more than apparent as the crowd belted it out with her from the opening number of *All I Really Want*. All the audience wanted Alanis delivered — and then some."

Even reviewers who have steadfastly searched for glitches in the performance have grudgingly admitted that she brings energy to her live performances. As Sun Media Corporation music critic John Sakamoto commented, "A curious thing seems to happen whenever someone reaches the dizzying level of commercial and cultural acceptance that Alanis Morissette has attained over the past 12 months. And that is, she finds herself in the dangerous position where the audience's response has very little to do with the quality of her performance. That scenario came into play Saturday night . . . as an adoring crowd of 35,000 fans packed Molson Park for the final show of Morissette's first Canadian tour as a bona fide headliner. Despite turning in a set during which she at times sounded on the verge of exhaustion, and at others veered dangerously close to rote, this country's biggest musical export since Bryan Adams had nothing to worry about. She had already won over the audience long before she even stepped on stage.

"Not that she crassly exploited the situation. . . . Morissette ran through a polished 16-song, 90-minute show that consisted of all of JAGGED LITTLE PILL plus three new songs, each of which can hold their own with virtually anything on that multi-platinum album. (Before the show, Morissette was presented with a diamond award, signifying sales of one million copies in Canada. The album is actually just 300,000 or so copies shy of hitting the two million mark.)" Of the three new songs, *King Of Intimidation, Can't Not,* and *No Pressure Over Cappuccino*, Sakamoto preferred the latter, "a moving ballad inspired by Morissette's twin brother, Wade, who preceded Alanis into the world by 12 minutes, but now faces the daunting task of following in her shadow for the rest of his life. *Can't Not*, which is also the name of Morissette's tour, has evolved into a darkly powerful anthem. Taken at a much more deliberate pace than it was earlier in the tour, it was the evening's most impressive showcase for her four-piece band, which has gelled into a remarkably precise unit."

Tales of her life on the road began to abound in the local press as Morissette and her band toured North America. "Arriving for a light lunch at Fresco, a midtown Tuscan restaurant near her hotel, Ms. Morissette appears cheerful, unpretentious and clear-eyed," reported writer Jon Pareles of *The New York Times*. "She's wearing a wool cap and a dark jacket over a glittery silver blouse; there's no makeup on her face. Sitting down, she asks a hovering waiter for a cup of throat-soothing chamomile tea; 'I'm a singer on the road,' she explains. . . . The waiter arrives to recite a list of specials, and Ms. Morissette brightens up at one: roasted onion and garlic soup. 'That's what I'm getting,' she says. 'I don't care who I offend with my breath.'"

Jon Beam of the *Minneapolis-St. Paul Star Tribune* summed it up by saying, "It's not easy being Alanis Morissette these days. She is the great female rock success story of the '90s, the champion of a new breed of young women whom *The New York Times* has described as uninhibited and smart, bruised and resilient, unorthodox and proud of it." Beam wanted to know, in the wake of all that, what motivated her. "My music and my evolution, not only as a writer but as a person," she said. "I'm excited about this whole journey, regardless of whether people follow all along. I'm fully aware of the fact this external success — No. 1 on the chart, Grammy nomination craziness — may not always be. It may come back, it may come in cycles, it may never come again. That's part of it I can't control. All I can say now is I'm going to be honest with where I'm at creatively."

In *Details* magazine Jeff Spurrier reported a somewhat more stereotypical tale of life on the road with a rock band. "'Did anyone get laid last night?' Alanis asks her band as the tour van pulls out of Seattle on the way to Vancouver. No one answers. This means that the high scorer in the band's unofficial one-night-stand league remains the current leader, with four bodies bedded. Whoever it is. 'I'm really proud of us,' Alanis chirps. She would be. Since finishing PILL, she's been making up for lost time, smoking joints and having one-night stands, whereas the other Alanis was a tower of self-control. Sort of. 'I never allowed myself to go off the path when I was younger,' she mutters. 'There are a lot of things I didn't do. I lost my virginity at nineteen but I was very sexually active since I was fourteen, doing everything but. Isn't that odd? I enjoyed what I was doing, but I couldn't fully enjoy it.'"

"Alanis is small and much prettier than she photographs," adds Spurrier, "with a wide, sensuous mouth that seems locked in a perpetual smile; large, engaging hazel-brown eyes and chest-length, curly auburn hair. . . .We meet the next morning for a late breakfast in a Vancouver coffee shop. Alanis is having fruit, a dry bagel, and chamomile tea. Still tired, she's wearing her trademark retro-'70s clothes, which look fresh out of the thrift-store bargain bin: candy-apple-red polyester bell-bottoms, Adidas sneakers, and an oversize men's shirt that covers her frame like a tent. . . . Later, in the lobby of the hotel where the band are staying," continues Spurrier, in the wake of a Toronto interviewer questioning whether people can ever truly evolve, "Alanis pauses at the elevator. 'There are a lot of people who resent success here,' she says quietly. 'If this was a confessional record that I released independently and it didn't succeed, you'd believe it. But because it's succeeding, you don't know whether to believe it or not.'"

As David Wild reported in *Rolling Stone*, "To stay sane on the road, Morissette reads, meditates, and exercises. Socially, she says, 'I've just been dating a whole bunch of people and kind of making up for lost time.' More chastely, she has made a habit of painting the fingernails of many of the men she encounters. She started with her own band mates and has moved onto other men she has met, including the members of Better Than Ezra.

'It's a good excuse to get a guy to put his hand on your knee,' she says."

What all of this amounts to is that there is something straightforward about Alanis Morissette which designates her as the heir of a previous generation of rock music artists and activists. And that is why there was an amazing symbolism in her performance in Hyde Park in London at the end of June 1996, a fund-raising concert for Prince Charles' Trust Charity. Organizers expected to raise about one million dollars through ticket and merchandise sales, and 150,000 people showed up for the concert featuring The Who's Roger Daltrey, John Entwistle, and Peter Townshend, as well as Bob Dylan and Eric Clapton, Ron Wood and Gary Glitter.

In a Canadian Press story, Helen Branswell reported on the central role Alanis Morissette assumed in this event. The organizers "felt her participation was key to attracting a younger audience that might not be drawn by Dylan or Clapton. . . . Morissette played a set of eight songs from her megahit album JAGGED LITTLE PILL, which won her four Grammys and has sold more than 12 million copies. Her set included hit singles *Hand In My Pocket, You Oughta Know* and *Ironic*. But it was on *Not the Doctor* and her finale, *You Learn,* that she really let rip, dancing like a dervish and joining her drummer for a frenzied drum duet."

In the world of rock, there is no ceremony to record officially any transfer of the baton from one generation of rock star to another. Perhaps the closest we come to seeing the inheritance of rock bequeathed took place at Hyde Park. Morissette is carrying on the traditions of rock music. Her work is rebellious and self-indulgent. And she is presenting a legitimate alternative vision and a way of living, not only for her generation but also for the previous generation of rock music fans who haven't achieved very much since The Who were Morissette's age "talkin' about" their generation.

The baton was passed, symbolically at least, at Hyde Park in the British sunshine. And in the months since that event, audiences have continued to show that Morissette is one of their chief leaders in a new rock movement which calls for some heady changes in society. Based on artistic integrity, legitimately expressed outrage, and the rebellious frankness of rock music itself, Alanis Morissette is leading the charge towards a personal emotional honesty which may lead to a concurrent rational social honesty as well.

It was almost too ironic that there was a ghost standing silently on the lawns at Hyde Park, a certain teacher named Kenneth Gorman who, years earlier, purchased Alanis' privately released single, *Fate Stay With Me* when she was only 12 years old. This ghost was the same man who had been in Hyde Park 21 years before, in the waning moments of another era, to witness the last major concert there in 1975. A few months after Morissette's Hyde Park performance, Gorman recalled her note to him while she was in elementary school. "Watch 4 me," she wrote. Gorman responded, "I will. As will the world."

CANADIAN
MUSICIAN
THE ALANIS MORISSETTE BAND
ONE SWEET GIG

Live at Hyde Park.

Hey everybody 9/18

I'm having such a damn good time on the road right now - seriously. We're off to Europe and we'll be back in November. I'll see you when I'm back

TAKE CARE OUT THERE

Love,
Alanis Morissette

·ten·

Head Over Feet

I know there are a million more [songs]. And a million more revelations and thoughts and confusions that I haven't even begun to write about yet.

— *Alanis Morissette*

I've never felt this healthy before
I've never wanted something rational
I am aware now
I am aware now

— *Head Over Feet*

It's January 29th, 1997.

Many of Canada's music journalists and executives have battled the traffic to drive downtown to the new Canadian Broadcasting Corporation (CBC) building for a news conference sponsored by the Canadian Academy of Recording Arts and Sciences (CARAS), where this year's nominees for its annual Juno Awards are to be announced, the winners to receive their prizes during a national television broadcast from the Copps Coliseum in Hamilton, Ontario on March 9.

It's an annual strawberry social without the strawberries. It's not the kind of press conference where anyone is regaled with intense questions. It's more like a large brunch time cocktail party, but without the cocktails, a chance for music media to mingle and argue, debate and snack on fresh fruit and dip with bagels. And if anyone there is surprised or patriotically pleased that Canadian music has rocketed into worldwide prominence, they're not going to say so. No, better to pretend that everyone knew it all along.

It's a low key event this year, almost as if Alanis Morissette's near sweep of awards and her dynamic performance at the Junos in 1996 is impossible to follow up. Granted Celine Dion is the big news this year with four Grammy nominations and six Juno nominations, another Canadian superstar who has become a household name in various corners of the world. But Dion has been around a while, doesn't come packaged in all that dismay which, a year earlier, still crinkled around Alanis Morissette. Dion is set to assume top billing from Morissette at this year's Juno celebration.

The only controversy, now that many people have given up on the argument over whether Morissette is legitimate or not, is the future of the people who work in the CBC building in which the press conference is housed. Morissette and a vast array of other talented female artists may be freely expressing their emotional outrage, but no one in Canada is yet getting very steamed up by CBC purges on the part of Canada's federal government, part of that new government ethic of cutting down on everything except computer information highway purchases and corporate tax breaks. But if anyone is worried about that this morning, they're not saying very much. It's the annual media soiree. It's time to meet your neighbor, gather up your press kit, hear a few words of national pride from CARAS president Lee Silversides, and view taped performances of some of the nominees.

Silversides announces a new Juno to be presented this year for special international achievements by Canadian musicians. "Celine Dion, Alanis Morissette and Shania Twain have made history around the world this year and we all watched with pride as each of their extraordinary career stories unfolded," says Silversides. "It is a natural extension of that pride, and the subsequent realization of just how far Canada's music industry has progressed, that the Academy pays tribute to the three artists who, with their success, have not only brought honor to themselves but to the whole Canadian music community." The Juno in question will be called the International Achievement Award.

What follows, in alphabetical order, is a brief profile of their achievements. Dion, for instance, has sales of her current album FALLING INTO YOU of more than 15 million copies. Twain's album, THE WOMAN IN ME, has become the best-selling album by a female country artist of all time, surpassing Patsy Cline's Greatest Hits album. Morissette is cited for selling more than 20 million copies of JAGGED LITTLE PILL worldwide. "Morissette," we are told, "who is nominated for two Grammys this year, has already picked up five Junos, four Grammys, two MTV Awards, a Brit Award in the United Kingdom, an Echo Award in Germany for her JAGGED LITTLE PILL CD and had her contribution to the video medium recognized at the 7th annual MuchMusic Video Awards with four awards as well as a special trophy from *Billboard* magazine in recognition of her international success."

In addition to the Juno award she will share with Dion and Twain, Morissette is nominated in two other categories this year as well, still for her work on JAGGED LITTLE PILL. She is nominated for Single of the Year for *Ironic* and in the category of Songwriter of the Year.

The year 1996 was certainly a remarkable one for Alanis Morissette, perhaps the most remarkable for any woman artist in the history of rock music. After ink stopped being spilled over the question of her artistic integrity, most of 1996 was spent keeping track of Morissette's various awards, the way JAGGED LITTLE PILL continued to break records as a multi-million selling album and even her status in critic polls.

Jane Stevenson of the *Toronto Sun* reported early in January 1996 that Morissette had done well in *Rolling Stone's* annual Critics' Poll. "In the January 25 issue, Morissette and fellow Canuck Neil Young are named Artists Of The Year behind the No. 1 choice, Britain's PJ Harvey. Morissette's *You Oughta Know* was named third best single of 1995, after Coolio's *Gangsta's Paradise* and Edwyn Collins' *A Girl Like You.* Meanwhile, in the accompanying Readers' Poll, Morissette came in third as Artist Of The Year after Live, and Hootie and The Blowfish. Interestingly, readers put her album, JAGGED LITTLE PILL, in both the Worst and Best Album categories. Similarly, *You Oughta Know* was the Number One Best Single, but also wound up in the Worst Single category. The readers liked her voice, though, naming Morissette the Best Female Singer and the Best New Female Singer," reported Stevenson.

The first true indication of Morissette's popular success outside the alternative music circle came February 28, 1996 when she won four Grammy Awards, breaking a Canadian record for one night's worth of Grammy hardware. She was joined in victory by fellow Canadians Shania Twain and Joni Mitchell. Morissette, nominated in six categories, won Album of the Year, Best Rock Song for *You Oughta Know*, Best Rock Album, and Best Female Rock Vocalist. "Then, in a purely Canadian moment," wrote Katherine Monk in the *Vancouver Sun* while recounting her reaction to one or other of these awards, "Morissette went on to give a typically Canadian humble pie acceptance speech: 'I accept this award for any one who has ever written an album from a spiritual and pure place. All I can say is I love you (producer) Glen (Ballard) and there's lots of room for other artists, there's no such thing as the best.'"

The Globe & Mail's Elizabeth Renzetti reported the four Grammys as well, noting, "She had been nominated for six awards, which was loudly touted as an indication that the Grammys were suddenly hip and no longer the 'Granny' awards. . . . While Ms. [Joni] Mitchell clutched her award and giddily babbled her thanks, Ms. Morissette, less than half Ms. Mitchell's age, accepted the rock vocalist prize with gravity. 'This doesn't represent that I'm better than the other women on the list,' she said."

Renzetti was also on hand for the Juno Awards in Canada less than a month later on March 10. "Alanis Morissette isn't just the poster girl for female *angst*, she's a walking advertisement for free trade," said Renzetti. "Last night she swept the Juno Awards in Hamilton, having pulled off a similar feat across the border at last month's Grammy Awards." Morissette's Junos included Single of the Year for *You Oughta Know*. She also won in the categories of Female Vocalist and Songwriter. JAGGED LITTLE PILL was awarded Album of the Year and Rock Album of the Year.

By late summer, Morissette was closing in on album-selling records held by rock's biggest names, all of which was gleefully reported in most Canadian media. Paul Cantin, in August, reported in the *Ottawa Sun* that Morissette could conceivably "join the all-time sales pantheon, next to Michael Jackson and The Eagles." He reported that JAGGED LITTLE PILL had sold 100,000 copies weekly since its release in June 1995, doubling that output for five weeks after the Grammy Awards and sometimes selling above the 100,000 copies per week level during other periods. A month later, in September, Canadian Press reported that the Recording Industry Association of America had announced sales of 12 million copies in the United States, tying her with Whitney Houston for best-selling album ever by a female solo artist. "The 12 million figure also doesn't include Canadian sales figures, which are close to two million, or her sales in other countries. The album continues to register in the Top 10 best-selling album charts in more than a dozen countries," Canadian Press announced in a syndicated article.

Also by late summer Morissette's reputation went super-nova in electronic space, with an average of over 1,000 information sites and home pages built in her honor on the World Wide Web monthly from June to December 1996, establishing for her an electronic presence unrivalled by any other musician in the world. Even more incredible is that this Alanis cult on the Web is completely spontaneous: in most cases, these 8,000 or more sites are the work of private individuals, using their own time and resources to pay homage to her music and character. Many of these sites are strikingly sophisticated in their manipulation of the media to create a tribute to their idol, while others like the PAAMM (People Against Alanis Morissette Music) site take idolatry lightly. Morissette's own official website (created by Reprise Records) is, however, a tiny, spare piece of work, displaying only a brief biographical note and a couple of photos. Ironically, Morissette *herself* is something of a net ghost. She has done only a handful of "chat" sessions with fans: when asked, "Is the net a common tool for you?" she responded, "I'm actually very apprehensive when it comes to technological evolution." This hasn't stopped the web feeding frenzy as chat about her music, her taste in booze, and her sex life continues to buzz at an ever increasing rate. Alanis Morissette may be the first bona fide 21st-century recording artist, one whose reputation has been built as much on her presence on the Internet as on her performances in live concerts and television videos.

Morissette has had her share of triumphs in the world of rock music videos. As her image, obscured and fuzzy throughout the video for *You Oughta Know,* gradually became clearer through the videos for *Hand In My Pocket, Head Over Feet, You Learn,* and *Ironic,* Morissette began to pick up nominations and hardware in this genre as well, despite her reticence to grant awards any recognition as a true measure of an artist's worth. The video for *Ironic* won two MuchMusic Awards in September 1996 for Best Video and Best International Video, while Morissette received a People's Choice Award for favorite female artist. In New York, she scored three victories at the 13th annual MTV Music Video Awards, including Best New Artist, and Best Female Video for *Ironic,* and, indirectly, Best Editing in a Video awarded to Scott Grey, again for *Ironic.*

Ironic the song and the video were then nominated in the New Year for Grammy Awards in the categories of Record of the Year and Best Musical Video, respectively, and Morissette again made a strong showing, best and worst, in the *Rolling Stone* Critic's Poll published in January 1997, not to mention her appearances in *Billboard* as Artist of the Year for 1996, on the the year-end celebrity list in *People,* and as the "'Ironic' Icon" on the cover of the annual issue of *Entertainment Weekly,* where she ranked as the Number 3 "Entertainer of the Year" behind Rosie O'Donnell and Mel Gibson. Ironic icon, perhaps, but most certainly the icon for the new movement of women artists in rock and pop music.

As the nominations for the 1997 Juno Awards unfolded during the press conference in Toronto, this movement became even more pronounced. Chantal Kreviazuk and Wendy Lands, both nominated under Best New Solo Artist, and Amanda Marshall, nominated for Female Vocalist of the Year and Single of the Year, joined forces with Dion, Twain, and Morissette.

Before and after the Juno nomination press conference, Alanis Morissette was the subject of some scuttlebutt, conjecture about here where-abouts and the release of a new album. No one, apparently, is sure if she will be at the Juno Awards in March. In fact, no one is sure if she has returned home from a reported holiday to Africa and India, her way of taking a vacation after bringing to a close her exhausting world tour at the end of 1996. Rumors abound that she is in Ottawa, visiting family and friends. There's an ambivalence surrounding any discussion of Morissette. She's still scooping up awards relating to her work on JAGGED LITTLE PILL, but this is going to be Celine Dion's year, primarily because Morissette has not yet released her follow-up album.

At the root of the ambivalence about what Morissette will do next is the calm in the wake of the storm. At the Juno press conference in the almost ghostly CBC building, so much is the same and so much is now different. Call it euphoria aftermath. Even the media detractors of Morissette are missing all the excitement. No one seems to want to sit down and bring into clearer focus the dreamlike state of knowing Morissette has sold more than 20 million albums, and, at the same time, appears to be everything that she has admitted she is. Better to wait and see. Strangely enough, if there is pressure on Alanis Morissette to somehow follow-up the extraordinary success of JAGGED LITTLE PILL, the pressure is secondary to that which rests on the shoulders of those who keep their jaundiced eye on the music scene. Everyone wants to be wrong or right, both at the same time. It's like betting your house on both teams in the Super Bowl. You can't win and you can't lose.

Prior to the end of 1996, it was reported that Morissette would return to the studio in January for an album to be released in April.

On the Internet, there was even an ongoing debate, testifying more to the fame of the artist and the size of her audience than actual accurate details, which suggested the new album would be entitled "FRET BORED." But in truth, Morissette has extended her time off early in 1997 and an album as early as April is entirely unlikely. Worse yet, the original plans for a second album in the spring from Maverick have been clearly delayed, so the wait is dragging on inexorably. Morissette knows what the second album means, yet she seems committed to approaching her next creation with the same straightforward artistic integrity which launched the work on JAGGED LITTLE PILL.

As Paul Cantin of the *Ottawa Sun* reported as early as March 1996, Morissette is aware of the pressure to release a successful follow-up to JAGGED LITTLE PILL. "There's obvious pressure. The next record, the poor thing, has to live up to this precedent," she said. "All I can promise is I'm going to write exactly where I'm at. I may lose a few people in my audience. Or I may gain some. Or not. I can't say. All I can say is I am going to be honest with where I'm at. And that will never change. In many ways, I really feel that I have only scratched the surface. I know there are a million more (songs). And a million more revelations and thoughts and confusions that I haven't even begun to write about yet." In light of the close collaborative relationship Morissette has with Glen Ballard and their mutual reports of an almost spiritual creativity together, announcements that Ballard will be involved with the next album are not surprising.

Fans at her concerts during the latter half of 1996 were treated to a possible preview of songs to appear on a new album. In his review of Morissette's "Can't Not" tour of Canada, John Sakamoto reported as far back as August 1996 that Morissette had been working new material into her concert sets. "Four songs in particular have popped up with some regularity and, if their quality is any indication of the follow-up to JAGGED LITTLE PILL, Morissette shouldn't have any worries about the dreaded sophomore slump. Or, for us Canadians, the 'difficult fourth album,' " he wrote.

Can't Not, says Sakamoto, is "the song after which Morissette's current Canadian tour is named. Apparently written as a reply to either a personal or professional detractor, it features a dramatic opening line — "I'd be lying if I said I was completely unscathed" — and some banshee-style wailing between choruses. Morissette has said she hasn't decided whether to make it part of the next album. Leaving it unrecorded would certainly be a shame. *No Pressure Over Cappuccino*: inspired by Morissette's twin brother, this lovely, ethereal ballad includes alternately biting and comforting lyrics and has some of the same feel as *Hand In My Pocket*. Beautiful," said Sakamoto.

He also cites two new songs, *King Of Intimidation* and one penned by Morissette with her back up band called, for the time being, *I Don't Know*. *King of Intimidation* is "the first fruit of a re-teaming early this year with Glen Ballard, her collaborator on JAGGED LITTLE PILL. An edgy, mid-tempo rocker that wouldn't sound at all out of place on PILL. *All hail the king of intimidation. I Don't Know*: Penned by the entire band during a soundcheck at the tail end of January this year, this dynamic rocker was so new when Morissette worked it into her set in New York City ten days later that she didn't even have a proper title for it," wrote Sakamoto. "Introduced with the shrugging moniker of *I Don't Know*, the song uses a days-of-the-week device — e.g. "Thursday night is not Thursday night / 'Til Chris has sex with his bass" — before climaxing in a chorus of "Hold off 'til the weekend."

Full sets of the lyrics to these songs have been broadcast by fans on the Internet and show clearly that Morissette will not disappoint her audience if these songs appear on a new album. Take, for example, the first stanza and chorus of *King of Intimidation:*

For you they live in a quiet monastery
For you they wear whatever you want them to
as long as it is short
They count to ten when you tell them how to drive
And when they're afraid they let you speak for them

All hail the King of Intimidation
Obeyer of Christian behavior

— *King of Intimidation*

The song is prefaced by spoken words from an old recording: "The women of the family seem to feel that they owe it to the men of the family to look relaxed, rested, and attractive at dinnertime." This voice of outrage is complemented by the "pscyhobabble" of *No Pressure Over Cappucino*:

And you're like a 90s Jesus
And you revel in your psychosis
How dare you?

You sample concepts like hors d'oeuvres
And you eat questions for dessert
And is it just me or is it hot in here?

And you're like a 90s Kennedy
And you're only a million years old
They can't fool you . . .

And they wonder why you're frustrated
And they wonder why you're so angry
Is it just me or are you set up

— *No Pressure Over Cappucino*

Another song performed in concert during 1996 was entitled *Death of Cinderella,* whose delivery recalls *Hand In My Pocket*:

I'm wise and ambitious
And angry and free
And smart and available
And sexy . . .

And this is the story of the death of Cinderella
She'd grow to be a maid if she couldn't find a fella
Who can use her
And it's all you could do not to tie her to the bed . . .

— *Death of Cinderella*

The song concludes with Morissette proclaiming, "I'm gonna grow to be a maid and I'll never find a fella . . . / And it's all you can do not to kick me in the ass."

Even looking ahead, there is still too much at this point to look *back* on. Without any conclusions, the press conference for the 1997 Juno Awards now complete, there is a drifting out of the auditorium and then out of the CBC building itself. Music goes on and so does the journalistic work that records it.

What will Morissette do next? As she has made so abundantly clear over the past couple of years. Exactly what is right for her. Exactly what is right for her audience.

Logotype from one of the thousands of sites dedicated to Alanis on the World Wide Web.

'Ironic' Icon from the cover of Entertainment Weekly *where Alanis ranked as the Number 3 Entertainer of the Year.*

·Afterword·

I've always been the kind of person that would rather write a book than read it, and write a song rather than listen to one, and have a conversation rather than watch one on TV.

— Alanis Morissette

Life has a funny, funny way of helping you out
Helping you out

— Ironic

If Alanis Morissette was a lawyer, defending herself as an artist, a woman, and a human being, her summation to the jury would probably take the form of the video for her song *Ironic*. Because this video, as much as anything she has done, in just a few moments of musical delight and apparent triumph, encapsulates the complexity of being an artist, a woman, and a human being with the challenge of trying to sustain these conditions in the face of harsh and unjust times. At the same time, this video probably sums up her own history and offers a peek into the future, from the standpoint of her personal psychological empowerment.

In the video, her self-confessed "duality" of character has multiplied itself by two. Filmed in a car, the mature Alanis is at the wheel, quite literally the mother of herself, keeping an eye on the other facets of her personality, her alter egos. There's the moody, introspective girl wearing a green sweater in the back seat who, though often quiet and thoughtful, isn't above throwing a tantrum. There's beside her the flirtatious, eccentric girl in yellow with braided hair, a Lolita who teases. And there's also the free-spirited girl wearing red in the front seat who has no sense of caution, the one who dangerously hangs out the window of the speeding car of life, purely for the irresponsible pleasure of it. But they all join in to deliver the chorus of *Ironic*, "Who would've thought . . . it figures" and the thematic point, "Isn't it ironic . . . don't you think." Yes, they all think it's ironic because, indeed, it's not that ironic at all.

The video testifies to the fact that Alanis Morissette has found herself, has grown comfortable with the various components of her personality which combine to be that *self*. And when the car runs out of gas and she stands outside at one with herself, there's a feeling of profound triumph over her circumstances. Because, in the sense that we are more than one series of personality traits, there is a lot for us to see about ourselves as we watch Alanis Morissette in this video. The story of Alanis Morissette becomes, in some small way, the story of all the inner conflicts most human beings endure on their way to wherever it is they are going.

As so many of her critics, fans, and musical peers have pointed out, something about Morissette's self-possession, clarity of intention, outspokenness, and integrity draws us to her, makes us want to root for her. She feels like David to us as he walks undaunted into the dusty valley to battle Goliath. We root for her and end up cheering for ourselves. The odds are stacked against us, outside of our control, and the various developments which impact on our lives, which control us much more than we like them to, are huge and complex and relentless. Yet something inside us wishes to walk into the valley without flinching, to take on this Goliath which, whether we recognize its specifics or not, wishes to trivialize our lives and disenfranchise us.

No wonder Morissette's JAGGED LITTLE PILL has struck such a resounding chord with an entire generation around the world. It's not just that we want to root for her, but that she conveys a comforting and forgivable self-indulgence in the act of rooting for ourselves. Each time she walks on stage to begin a concert, she tells the story of her life. And each time, a tremendous empathy takes place because her story is, essentially, our story as well. She tells candidly her story of precocious ambition, the impact of forces, first parental and then social, which sometimes steer us where we do not want to go. And she tells about psychological empowerment, about knowing ourselves, about the state of integrity which lies on the other side of this self-awareness like a gleaming pasture on the other side of a fence. And we see ourselves in all of that progression. We know what it feels like. We know what we want to believe, even when so many would convince us there's little worth believing in at all.

We all don't get to be Alanis Morissette. We all don't get to enjoy such a close proximity to our audience and that fulfilling feeling of solidarity which empathy always precedes. But we do get the fulfilment knowing someone who does. We all don't make the psychological journey she's made at such a young age. For some of us it takes much longer. We certainly all don't manage to succeed the way she has as a result of bringing integrity to our creativity. We all don't even opt to be so active — "I've always been the kind of person that would rather write a book than read it, and write a song rather than listen to one, and have a conversation rather than watch one on TV," she has stated — but we nonetheless prefer being active to passivity.

On the surface of it, the story of Alanis Morissette would seem to be the story of Alanis Morissette only. From childhood to teenage pop queen through psychological empowerment and creative integrity to superstar. And in the way that history isn't finished yet, her story isn't finished yet either. But, in truth, the story of Alanis Morissette is much more than her story. It's the story of a generation and, to a lesser extent, the generation which preceded it. It's the story of the continuing evolution of rock music, an evolution which, at the same time, maintains its historic principles of rebellion and creative self-indulgence, its ritual tendency to be blunt, to be outraged and outrageous, its persistent facility for mirroring the social, cultural, political, and economic forces which affect all of us day to day, not to mention how we respond to these forces.

Within the framework of this larger story, the story of Alanis Morissette intrigues us because of the variety and intensity in the performances of her musical peers, because of the jagged honesty she radiates herself, and, more importantly, because millions of people have connected with her work. There is more than a hint of potential revolution in the size and scope of this kind of relationship between artist and audience. It makes one consider that the contest is now once again afoot. On one side of the field there is the seasoned and manipulated cynicism which has so entrenched an entire generation in what we call the age of irony. This team will try to score its points by diffusing hope into nothing more than superficial trend. On the other side of the field is the bedraggled underdog of inherent human faith in positive change, a David finding inspiration in candid music which can sow the seeds of gentle rebellion. This team will try to acknowledge and then maintain a solidarity in its quest for human social improvement. This is the age-old contest which has always been underway, though never before against such a colossal machine of greedy self-interest.

None of us know where all of this new solidarity is headed. Perhaps nowhere very much different. Perhaps some place profoundly encouraging and profoundly individual. It isn't a war per se. It's just trying to be yourself, even when overwhelming forces want you to be someone else. And most of all, if there is an alternative to all that assails us on the eve of a new millennium, part of that alternative is human faith that everything is going to be all right. Fittingly, the last word belongs to Alanis Morissette:

What it all comes down to
Is that everything's gonna be quite alright . . .
What it all comes down to
Is that I haven't got it all figured out just yet . . .
I've got one hand in my pocket
And the other one is giving the peace sign . .

ALANIS

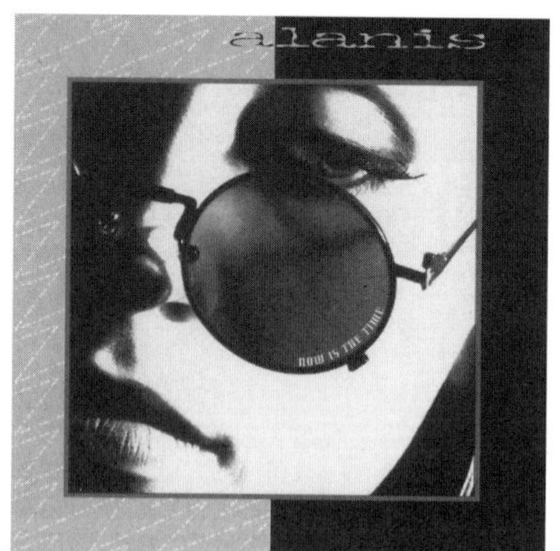
alanis
NOW IS THE TIME

·Discography·

ALBUMS

ALANIS 1991
MCA Records (Canada) MCAD-10253

Feel Your Love / Too Hot / Plastic / Walk Away / On My Own / Superman / Jealous / Human Touch / Oh Yeah! / Party Boy

NOW IS THE TIME 1992
MCA Records (Canada) MCAD-10731

Real World / An Emotion Away / Rain / The Time Of Your Life / No Apologies / Can't Deny / When We Meet Again / Give What You've Got / (Change Is) Never A Waste Of Time / Big Bad Love

JAGGED LITTLE PILL 1995
Maverick Records 9 45901-2

All I Really Want / You Oughta Know / Perfect / Hand In My Pocket / Right Through You / Forgiven / You Learn / Head Over Feet / Mary Jane / Ironic / Not The Doctor / Wake Up

SPACE CAKES (Acoustic) 1995

Head Over Feet / Right Through You / Forgiven / Perfect / Not the Doctor / You Learn

SINGLES

Fate Stay With Me *1986*
Too Hot *1991*
Feel Your Love *1991*
Walk Away *1991-92*
Plastic *1992*
An Emotion Away *1992-93*
No Apologies *1993*
Real World *1993*
(Change Is) Never A Waste Of Time *1993*

You Oughta Know *1995*
You Oughta Know (album version) / You Oughta Know (Jimmy the Saint blend) / Perfect (acoustic version) / Wake Up

Hand In My Pocket (1) 1996
Hand In My Pocket / Head Over Feet (live acoustic) / Not The Doctor (live acoustic)

Hand In My Pocket (2) 1996
Hand In My Pocket / Right Through You (live acoustic) / Forgiven (live acoustic)

You Learn (1) 1996
You Learn / Your House (live in Tokyo) / Wake Up (live version) / Hand In My Pocket

You Learn (2) 1996
You Learn (album version) / You Oughta Know (live Grammy Awards version)

Head Over Feet 1996
Head Over Feet / You Learn (live version) / Hand In My Pocket (live version) / Right Through You (live version)

Ironic (1) 1996

Ironic (album version) / Forgiven (live version) / Not The Doctor (live acoustic version) / Wake Up (live acoustic version)

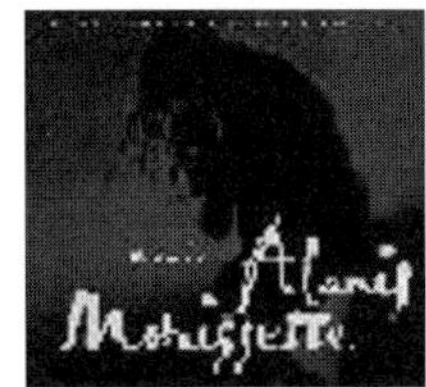

Ironic (2) 1996

Ironic / You Oughta Know (live Grammy Awards version) / Mary Jane (live version) / All I Really Want (live version)

All I Really Want 1996

All I Really Want / Ironic (live version) / Hand In My Pocket (live version)

BOOTLEG ALBUMS

Intellectual Intercourse: In Concert and Beyond (Germany) 1995
Erotica (Milwaukee) 1995
Quite Alright (Baden Baden) 1995
Rockin' The Ford (Hollywood) 1995
The Girl With The Thorn In Her Side (London, England) 1995
Miss Thing (Amsterdam) 1995
Hard To Swallow (Los Angeles, Germany, Amsterdam) 1995
The Girl Can't Help It (Germany) 1995
Roseland (New York City) 1996
Eyes Of A Child (Munich, London, Rome) 1996
Going North
Tune In, Turn On, Drop Out
What Comes Around
Who's That Girl
Universally Yours
I've Never Been In Love

·Bibliography·

Abraham, Carolyn & Provencher, Norman. "Fate Stay With Me." *Ottawa Citizen*, February 24, 1996.

Aizlewood, John. "Alanis Morissette: She's Got The Whole World In Her Hands." *Q*, August 1996.

Anonymous. "Jagged Little Pill Ties Sales Record." *Reuter-Canadian Press*, September 11, 1996.

Anonymous. "Alanis Scores A Hat Trick At MTV Awards." *Canadian Press*, September 5, 1996.

Anonymous. "Rave Review Down Under For Canada's Morissette." *Canadian Press*, May 1, 1996.

Anonymous. "Frenzied Fans Welcome Morissette." *Canadian Press*.

Anonymous. "The Muse Interview: Sara McLachlan." *Best of Muse*, www.val.net, 1995.

Anonymous."Tori's Story," *Hot Wired*, 1992.

Anonymous. "On The Edge," *KPOI 97.5*, August 6, 1995.

Anonymous. "Coming Of Age." *People Weekly*, March 4, 1996.

Anonymous. "Alanis Morissette." *People Weekly*, December 30, 1996.

Anonymous. "A Genial Morissette Keeps Her Anger in Her Pocket." *Boston Globe*, February 1996.

Bauder, David. "Women Artists Dealing With The Shadow of Morissette." *Associated Press*, August 11, 1996.

Beam, Jon. "Morissette At Ease With Success." *Dayton Daily News*, March 11, 1996.

Bliss, Karen. "The Alanis Morissette Band: One Sweet Gig." *Canadian Musician*, June 1996.

Bliss, Karen. "Alanis Morissette." *Canadian Musician*, October 1995.

Block, Francesca Lia. "Tori Amos: The Volcano Lover." *Spin*, March 1996.

Bourrie, Mark. "Ottawans Not All Keyed in to Morissette." *Toronto Star*, March 5, 1996.

Branswell, Helen. "Morissette Helps Rock Hyde Park." *Canadian Press*, June 30, 1996.

Brown, Mark. "The Jagged Edge of Fame." *Edmonton Journal*, August 2, 1996.

Cantin, Paul. "Alanis' Next Move: After Jagged Little Pill, What Can She Do For An Encore." *Ottawa Sun*, August 8, 1996.

Cantin, Paul. "Morissette Closes In On The Boss, The Eagles." *Ottawa Sun*, August 23, 1996.

Cantin, Paul. "What You Oughta Know." *Ottawa Sun*, www.canoe.ca, 1996.

Considine, J.D. "Morissette's Songs Sport 'Jagged' Edge." *Chicago Sun-Times*, March 1, 1996.

Corliss, Richard. "Viva The Divas!" *Time*, August 12, 1996.

Courtney, Kevin. "Rock's Ironic Icon For Women Strikes A Raw Nerve At SFX." *Irish Times*, April 23, 1996.

Decker, Shelly. "Mad About Alanis." *The Express*, August 1, 1996.

Di Perna, Alan. "Alanis-Smells Like Team Spirit-Morissette." *Guitar World Online*, September, 1996.

Evans, Paul, Futterman, Steve, et al. "Tori Amos." *The New Rolling Stone Encyclopedia of Rock & Roll,* New York: Rolling Stone Press, 1995.

——. "Paul Anka." *The New Rolling Stone Encyclopedia.*

——. "Kate Bush." *The New Rolling Stone Encyclopedia.*

——. "Sheryl Crow." *The New Rolling Stone Encyclopedia.*

——. "The Doors." *The New Rolling Stone Encyclopedia.*

——. "Marianne Faithfull." *The New Rolling Stone Encyclopedia.*

———. "PJ Harvey." *The New Rolling Stone Encyclopedia.*

——. "Hole." *The New Rolling Stone Encyclopedia.*

——. "Joni Mitchell." *The New Rolling Stone Encyclopedia.*

——. "Patti Smith." *The New Rolling Stone Encyclopedia.*

——. "The Sugarcubes/Bjork." *The New Rolling Stone Encyclopedia.*

Farley, Christopher John. "You Oughta Know Her." *Time Magazine,* February 26, 1996.

Fischer, Nathalie-Roze. "Passing Notes With Bjork: A Study of Human Behaviour." *Best of Muse,* www.val.net, 1996.

Fox, Marisa. "Alanis Has Crowd in Her Pocket, Mad Morissette Is All The Rage at Roseland." *New York Daily,* February 8, 1996.

Giles, Jeff. "You Oughta Know Her." *Newsweek,* August 7, 1995.

Gorman, Kenneth. "Hitting G Sharp: I Remember Alanis." *The Whig-Standard,* November 30, 1996.

Gundersen, Edna. "Will '95 Pop Queens Have Staying Power?" *USA Today,* February 25, 1996.

Hannaham, James. "Alanis in Wonderland." *Spin.* November 1995.

Hochman, David. "Best of 1996: Alanis Morissette." *Entertainment Weekly,* January 3, 1997.

Howell, Peter. "Alanis In Wonderland." *Toronto Star,* February 18, 1996.

——. "Alanis, We Hardly Knew Ya." *Toronto Star,* November 23, 1995.

——. "Queen Alanis." *Calgary Herald,* February 24, 1996.

Jackson, Rick. "One to One." *The Canadian Encyclopedia of Rock, Pop &*

Folk Music, Kingston: Quarry Press Inc., 1994.

Jenkins, Mark. "Sheryl Crow: 'Sheryl Crow'." *Washington Post*, September 25, 1996.

Jennings, Nicolas. "Adventures of Alanis in Wonderland." *Maclean's*, December 11, 1995.

Joyce, Jane. "The Fans of Alanis." *Montreal Gazette*, August 4, 1996.

Leiby, Richard. "Now THIS Is Ironic; It's Like A Hit Song That Got The Words Wrong." *Washington Post*, April 4, 1996.

LePage, Mark. "Why Alanis?" *Montreal Gazette*, August 3, 1996.

Livingstone, Barb. "Critic Abandons Job For Pop Star." *Calgary Herald*, August 1992.

Margolis, Lynne. "Morissette's Jagged Show Rocks Campus." *Pittsburgh Tribune*, February 1996.

McIlroy, Anne. "Rocker Morissette Returns to Frosty Canadian Roots." *The Globe & Mail*, March 9, 1996.

McLeod, Tyler. "She Came, We Saw, She Happened." *Calgary Sun*, August 3, 1996.

Melhuish, Martin. *Oh What A Feeling: A Vital History of Canadian Music*. Kingston: Quarry Press Inc., 1996.

Millea, Holly. "True Love?" *Premiere*, February 1997.

Monk, Katherine. "Grammy Night In Canada." *Vancouver Sun*, February 29, 1996.

Moon, Tom. "Brooding Morissette Writes Songs of Purposeful Anguish." *Houston Chronicle*, August 25, 1995.

Morse, Steve. "He Oughta Know; Coming Off His Work With Alanis Morissette, Glen Ballard Is As Hot As A Producer Can Be." *Boston Globe*, March 31, 1996.

Muretich, James. "'It's Like . . . Wow! I Love It!'" *Calgary Herald*, July 11, 1991.

Nicholls, Stephen. "Ottawa Teen Riding High." *Winnipeg Free Press*, November 6, 1991.

Pareles, Jon. "At Lunch With: Alanis Morissette." *New York Times*, February 28, 1996.

Piltz, Albrecht. "Screams and Whispers." *Keyboards*, June 1992.

Powers, Ann. "Holy Roller Joan Osborne Finds Salvation In God And Good Sex." *Rolling Stone*, March 21, 1996.

Provencher, Norman. "Conquering The World One Song At A Time." *Ottawa Citizen*, August 8, 1996.

——. "Alanis a Hit Everywhere Except Hometown Radio." *Ottawa Citizen*, August 19, 1995.

——. "Homecoming Queen: Alanis Morissette Formula Starting To Wear A Little Thin." *Ottawa Citizen*, August 10, 1996.

Powell, Betsy. "Canadians Strong On Grammys." *Canadian Press*, January 8, 1997.

Renzetti, Elizabeth. "Canadian Women Win Six Grammys." *The Globe & Mail*, February 29, 1996.

——-. "You Oughta Know: Morissette Sweeps Junos." *The Globe & Mail*, March 11, 1996.

——-. "Shery Crow: The Fun's Over." *The Globe & Mail*, December 26, 1996.

——-. "XX Marks The Spot." *The Globe & Mail*, January 11, 1997.

Sakamoto, John. "Alanis' New Songs." *Sun Media Corporation*, www.canoe.ca, August 8, 1996.

Sakamoto, John. "Alanis Can't Lose." *Sun Media Corporation*, www.canoe.ca, August 11, 1996.

Salutin, Rick. "CBC's Spectrum of Voices Will be Thinned to a Narrow Band." *The Globe & Mail*, December 20, 1996.

Saxberg, Lynn. "Teenage Fans Admire Singer's Unique Style And Tough Attitude." *Ottawa Citizen*, August 10, 1996.

——-. "Canadian Women Music's New Wave." *Toronto Star*, January 6, 1997.

Shuster, Fred. "Hit Maker And Record Breaker." *Vancouver Sun*, July 27, 1996.

Snyder, Julene. Untitled. *Bam*, July 20, 1995.

Spurrier, Jeff. "The People's Courtenay." *Details*, October 1995.

Stevenson, Jane. "Morissette High In Rolling Stone Polls." *Toronto Sun*, January 8, 1996.

——-. "Morissette Conquering Superstar." *Toronto Sun*, August 11, 1996.

——-. "Pop Queens Reign As Cover Girls." *Toronto Sun*, August 9, 1996.

——-. "The Buzz Is Hot On 23-Year-Old Toronto Singer Amanda Marshall." *Toronto Sun*, January 14, 1996.

——-. "Bonham's Burdens." *Toronto Sun*, March 20, 1996.

Sutcliffe, Phil. "The Ever Popular Tortured Artist Effect." *Mojo Magazine*, July 1996.

Varga, George. "And Now, The Best of Grammy's Quips and Trips." *San Diego Union-Tribune*, March 6, 1996.

Wild, David. "The Adventures of Miss Thing." *Rolling Stone*, November 2, 1995.

·Acknowledgments·

Special thanks to MCA Records (Universal Music) Canada, Warner Music Canada Ltd., CANAPRESS, and CARAS (Canadian Academy of Recording Arts and Sciences) for supplying photographs. For their silent archival research assistance, special thanks to the 20,000 or more creators and keepers of "Alanis" sites on the World Wide Web, including the remarkable sites at *Alanis Morissette Net, Miss Thing Web Site, Eric's Guide to Alanis Morissette, Isn't It Ironic . . . Don't You Think, Larry Brooks Home Page, Jagged Little Web Site, Alanis@legendinc, You Oughta Know Alanis Morissette, PAAMM, Alanis! Home Page,* and *Ticara's Home Page with Stuff about Alanis Morissette.* Without the extraordinary research skills of Michael Dawber, as well as his sense of humor, this book could not have been written.

And a personal thank you to Nancy Warnica for spontaneous research skills, thoughtful reading study, affection, patience and love during the writing of this book.